Cult Bees
& Legends

For Jo, Seb & Darcey

Cult Bees and Legends
Volume One

Author David Lane

Published by
Woodpecker Multimedia
Suite 6
2 St Johns Road
Hampton Wick
KT1 4AN

Tel (020) 8 255 6560
E-mail woodpeckermultimedia@hotmail.com
Web www.cultstarsandlegends.co.uk

ISBN: 0-9543682-0-7

Printed and bound in the United Kingdom

Introduction

Welcome to the first volume of what will hopefully prove to be a fascinating series of publications in which Brentford supporters are given the chance to reminisce with the most respected and highly regarded Brentford players from days gone by - along with some real characters and cult terrace heroes.

This book covers some of the major events in Brentford's post-war history and talks directly to players and personalities who were involved in the numerous promotions, relegations, cup runs, play-offs and bust-ups which are ingrained in all our memories.

Brentford Football Club may not have been the most successful of clubs down the years, but it has a great tradition of unearthing some fantastic talent and is a very proud and friendly club. Few players leave with anything other than happy memories of the Club, Griffin Park or its supporters and this special relationship was further underlined while researching the book.

But in days gone by fans often had no idea what players thought, what went through their minds when they were on the pitch or what the atmosphere was like in the dressing room. Once upon a time interviews with footballers divulged nothing more than what their favourite pre-match meal consisted of, or whether they preferred Billy Joel or Elton John while relaxing with their bottle of Blue Nun at home after the game. The following 160 pages will demonstrate how times have changed and how open and honest footballers can be if they're asked the right questions.

So who has been included in Volume One and why? Some of the star names will need no introduction to the majority of Brentford fans and were obvious inclusions, others were loyal servants of the club from more far off days and will be fondly remembered by those slightly older Bees amongst us. Some players have simply been tracked down and quizzed to establish the real story behind specific incidents or to clear up a juicy bit of terrace folklore.

As the book's title suggests, we've tracked down some really important Brentford stars from the past fifty years. Players like Terry Hurlock - whose crunching tackles were every bit as entertaining as his undoubted footballing skills - and Dean Holdsworth, whose goals took Brentford to the Third Division Championship in 1992.

I also braved the national rail network and travelled up to the North East to visit the highly colourful Joe Allon, who became Brentford's record transfer when we bought him from Chelsea in 1993. Allon's scoring record at Brentford was more impressive than a lot of people gave him credit for at the time, 29 goals from 55 games. Joe gives his views on a roller-coaster era at Brentford, which spanned The Bees relegation from Division One and the early David Webb days.

There's Andy Feeley, who formed a pivotal and intimidating part of Steve Perryman's promising Bees team that marched through to the Quarter Finals of the FA Cup at Anfield in 1989 where 44,000 fans saw Brentford finally eliminated by Liverpool. The Bees dispatched of high-flying Manchester City and Blackburn Rovers en-route to Anfield and Feeley looks back at some of his personal highlights from that record breaking cup run and shares his enlightened views on the future of the game now that he is Bury Football Club's Director of Youth.

Andy McCulloch is another terrace idol who was delighted to be given the chance to recall some great times at Griffin Park. Andy's goal-scoring partnership with Steve Phillips in the late seventies won The Bees promotion and the club a lot of new fans during an exciting era. McCulloch is another who certainly fits the Cult Bee bill, as any fan who recalls the Royal Oak stand will gladly testify.

There are also some real Griffin Park stalwarts included too. Players like Ken Coote, Tommy Higginson and Alan Nelmes who between them clocked up more than 1300 matches for The Bees and showed the kind of loyalty to the club that is unlikely to be matched again.

Ken Coote's record was amazing and he is a true club legend. Coote amassed 559 first team appearances for Brentford between 1949 and 1964 and was never booked once. Higginson was another player with an amazing record and averaged around forty games per season while he was at the club which spanned more than ten years.

Regular readers of the Brentford fanzine Beesotted will have hopefully enjoyed the interviews I have conducted with countless Bees players and managers over the past twelve years, but in this book, I have at last been able to dedicate the time and space that some of our finest players deserve. Beesotted has provided a great vehicle to interview players and has been instrumental, I feel, in helping change attitudes and standards in Brentford's publications.

The fanzine movement, which was at its height in the early 1990s, broke moulds within football and the humour and honesty that fan's magazines injected has made following our wonderful game more enjoyable. Regular football fans can now ask the questions they want answering and publish their work independently and even form groups capable of gaining control and running the football clubs they follow.

It must be said that the club have been fantastic in assisting me whenever I've needed their help during the production process and the healthy relationship I've forged with club officials has proved that they value positive input from the fans.

I hope Brentford supporters of all ages enjoy what has been a hugely enjoyable project for me to have managed during summer 2002. If the book is a success and raises a healthy amount for both Brentford Football Club and Bees United (the Supporters' Trust) in the process, then there should be another volume produced during 2003.

David Lane

Thanks to: Paul Slattery, Jim Levack, Dan Jackson, Gary Hargraves, Peter Gilham, Mark Chapman, Lee Doyle, Ray Chudley, John Lyons, Martin Holland, Greville Waterman and all the players featured in Cult Bees and Legends Volume One.

Photo credits are printed on page 158. Every effort has been made to trace the copyright holders of the photographs in this book - some have been unreachable. We would be grateful if the photographers concerned would contact us.

Contents

Ken Coote leads The Bees flying lesson

Ken Coote

Date: Monday July 30th, 2002
Venue: Ken's house, Whitton, Middlesex
Era: 1949-1964 Appearances: 559 Goals: 15

Loyalty is a rare commodity in today's game - players change football clubs almost as often as they change their socks - as agents chase the next signing-on fee, big-buck transfer or Bosman rule loop-hole.

Ken Coote certainly played in a very different era, the players' maximum wage restricted what footballers could earn, which for players like Ken made for a very different outlook on life compared to their modern day counterparts.

A strictly loyal, one club man, Coote amassed 559 games for Brentford and unbelievably never got booked once. Surely this is a record that will never be equalled?

Former Brentford manager, Jackie Gibbons, brought Ken to Griffin Park in the summer of 1949, snatching the Wembley Town winger from under the noses of First Division Burnley. Ron Greenwood tipped Gibbons off about Coote's availability and Brentford made one of the most significant signings in its history.

It took Ken a few seasons to fully establish himself, but following Tommy Lawton's arrival as Brentford manager in 1953, Coote's became one of the first names on the team sheet every week and eventually part of the very fabric of the football club itself.

Coote's devotion to The Bees arguably cost the player the chance of achieving greater honours in football - he was chosen to represent London in the original inter-cities European Fairs Cup and several First Division clubs made enquiries about the player - but Coote was happy to stay a local lad and has no regrets about sticking with Brentford through thick and thin.

Ken is a very unassuming man and seems almost underwhelmed by his remarkable achievements - but after some gentle prompting by his wife, Coote was coaxed into recalling some amazing memories from a time when Brentford F.C. were still a big force in London Football.

You joined Brentford in 1949 from Wembley where you were an amateur. It must have been a big jump in standards as The Bees had only recently been relegated from the First Division and we still had a lot of star players at the club?

"Well it was a very big step up, yes. Brentford were still a very good Second Division team at the time. Ron Greenwood's father recommended me to Brentford and I was very happy to come to Griffin Park. I'd just finished my National Service and I'd started working with my dad, just doing removals and that, so to then get the chance of becoming a full time footballer, it was a dream come true."

Did it change your life?

"I suppose it must have done yes, Brentford were a big club. My first league game was against Tottenham Hotspur at Griffin Park and there were over 30,000 people there. We lost, but it was terrific. Just before that game I played for Brentford's reserves away at West Ham and all my friends came to watch me play, they were all really excited for me."

You signed for Jackie Gibbons, the manager who succeeded the great Harry Curtis. What was he like as a man?

"He was very strict, a disciplinarian. But when you got used to him he was okay."

What was his training regime like then, tough?

"Yes it was very hard. We had to go in most days and train on the pitch at Griffin Park, but we did a lot of running around the streets and over in the parks around the town. Training was only ever between ten o'clock and midday though. We were only in for a couple of hours."

So was it straight in the pub afterwards?

"[Laughs] Sometimes, yes! The players nearly all drank and smoked back then. I still smoke today, not too many though."

You got your first goal for Brentford at Ewood Park, Black-

burn, scoring after just twenty seconds. You seemed to score quite regularly in the early years?

"Well I started at inside-forward at first and gradually worked my way backward, but I did like to attack. My career at Brentford didn't really get going until about 1953 though. Before then I was in and out of the team."

You began to establish yourself more after the legendary Tommy Lawton arrived. Obviously he spotted your potential straight away and you became an ever present from then on.

"Tommy Lawton was still a very good player when he joined and everyone knew of him. He was a household name back then. Tommy moved me to wing-half and that started things off for me at Brentford really."

The switch seemed to work very well as many fans that have been supporting the club for some years consider you the best full-back Brentford have ever had. But how would you fancy playing as wing-back as the players do these days?

"I'd have really liked that I think. Even though I played most of my career as a defender, I didn't like playing full back much and liked to be able to attack and get forward at wing-half."

What was Lawton like when things started to go wrong, he may have been a massive name, but he certainly wasn't a success at Griffin Park was he? We got relegated at the end of his first season.

"Well I thought Tommy Lawton was always a bit distant from the players really. He wasn't really a hands on manager. I think he picked the team on match days but he didn't seem too involved from day to day."

Looking back at the record books Brentford were still pretty high profile and we were invited to play against Celtic up in Glasgow and a couple of times in Holland against the Dutch national side. They must have been special days?

"The crowds were huge over in Holland, over 60,000. We did

2002– Coote at home in Whitton

Coote goes up for a header

alright too. It was a really big game for us. The Dutch weren't quite the great side they became, but they were still a very good team and it was an honour for Brentford to be asked to play them. I was also invited to represent London in the Fairs Cup which was an inter-cities competition back then [the cup was subsequently renamed Uefa Cup and became a club competition]. It was a real compliment. In fact the call-up was possibly my biggest achievement in the game. I was brought in to replace Danny Blanchflower who was the Captain of Northern Ireland at the time and playing for Tottenham. He was injured and I was invited to take his place. Brentford played over in Iceland too, in Reykjavik. I remember they didn't like us much over there and the fans hit us as we were coming off of the pitch... it was worse than Millwall. We also had a pre-season tour of Sweden where we played a team managed by Dai Hopkins, who played for Brentford in the First Division."

Your record at Brentford is pretty amazing when you think about it, the games in which you played for The Bees constitute almost one tenth of the total games the club has ever played.

"Well, you just carried on playing and that was it really. I don't think I looked at it as a really big thing when I was playing. Other people made more of the fact than I did."

Your total was 559 games in a Brentford shirt, but which one stands out most in your memory now?

"Playing up at Newcastle in the F.A. Cup Fourth round in 1955. I remember I had to mark Jackie Milburn and the crowd was very big. I can remember people calling out 'Wor Jackie' as I was running down the wing with him. Brentford did well in that game, we gave a good account of ourselves. We lost [3-2], but only just. It was a very big occasion for the club and the players."

Your career spanned four Brentford managers, but who do you feel was the best boss while you were at the club?

"I'd say Malcolm McDonald I think. He was a very good man-

Ken Coote & Johnny Rainford prepare for their testimonial match

"John Rainford used to say I was the best tackler going and couldn't figure out how I did it..."

ager, but I got on really well with everyone I played for at Brentford really."

The record books also show that in your 559 games you never received one booking... How can that be true of a defender?

"[Laughs] Well so they say... I don't think I was ever booked, but my wife says she remembers one. I can't though."

Do you think you had to do a lot more to get booked back then or was your timing that perfect?

"Well it's ridiculous these days. Some of the things people get booked for aren't real bookings. John Rainford used to say I was the best tackler going and couldn't figure out how I did it... he said I always went in and came out with the ball... "

Like a lot of Brentford players from the 50s and 60s, you still live within a few miles of Griffin Park. Do you get together with any of your old team mates now and again?

"Yes, I still see quite a lot of Jim Towers, George Bristow and Dennis Heath, they're just round the corner really and we keep in contact. I used to see a lot of John Rainford too but he died quite recently. A lot of the players lived around here because the club used to provide housing and the players would buy them from the club. Most of the players started off in club flats then moved up. I bought this house from Jack Dunnett, the ex-Brentford Chairman, but before me, Jimmy Hill, Wally Bragg and Billy Dare all lived here."

Everyone locally would have supported Brentford back then, so you must have been recognised every time you went out?

"[Laughs] People still come up and say hello even now, a lot of Brentford fans walk over to me when I'm out and about. It's really nice after all this time."

In today's climate I can't imagine that your Brentford record will ever be bettered. Jamie Bates was on track to topple it

a few years ago, but he moved to Wycombe. There aren't any real contenders these days are there?

"I think Ijah Anderson is a good player, when I saw him he impressed me. I thought he has got what it takes to go on and become one of the club's top players."

Looking back at your long and distinguished career, you played virtually every team in the league, played at almost every ground in the country and against some of the biggest names in the game. But you only have one medal to show for it, Brentford's Fourth Division Championship in 1963. Do you ever regret not moving on to see what you could have won elsewhere instead of staying with just one club?

"No, never. I never thought like that. I was happy at Brentford and we are local people and have always lived locally. At one stage Bill Dodgin (Snr) told me that Arsenal and West Brom had asked about me though, but nothing ever came of it."

When was the last time you got down to watch Brentford?

"I didn't get down at all last season I'm afraid [2001-02] but I do try and go to Griffin Park a few times per season normally. The club does phone me and whenever I want to go to a game there are always two tickets waiting for me. They've always been very good to me."

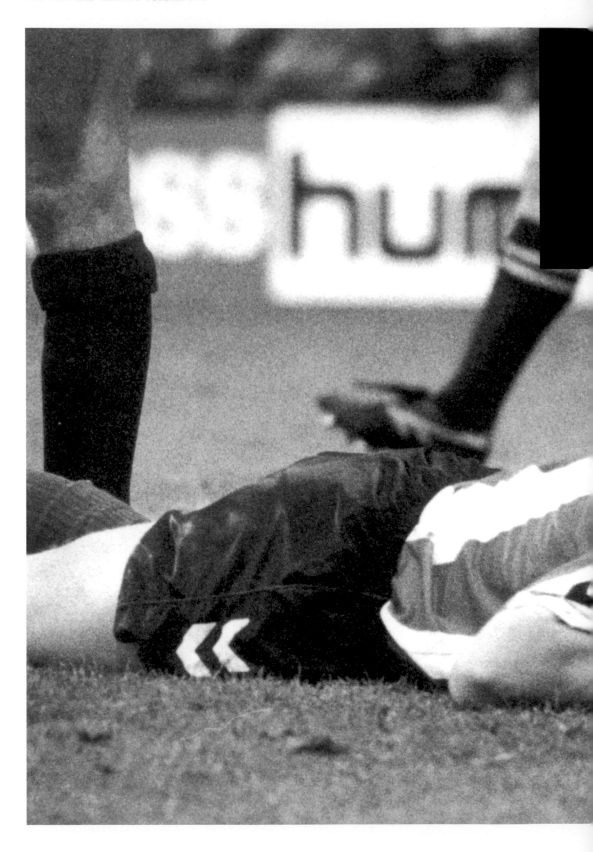

Joe Allon

Date: Thursday April 25th, 2002
Venue: Pelaw Stadium, Chester-Le-Street
Era: 1992-1994 Appearances: 55 Goals: 29

Joe's memory of his time at Brentford is pretty impressive; in fact it's almost photographic. It is also clear that he enjoyed his time at the club and that his days living in London, with the infamous Vinny Jones and Denis Wise, were the time of his life.

As a young footballer playing for Chelsea, and then as Brentford's record signing in the First Division, Joe was pretty high profile, especially when you consider his drinking partners were Messrs. Jones and Wise.

Joe still keeps in close contact with his former Blues buddies and admits to bursting into tears when Wise made him his testimonial guest of honour at his Stamford Bridge benefit match.

Allon was also invited along to Wise's *This Is Your Life* appearance. Geordie Joe could talk for hours about the laughs they have both shared down the years, but ominously admits that very few are actually printable.

Apparently Denis is too well connected to upset! The funny thing is that every time Joe mentions Wise or Vinny he automatically drops his broad Geordie accent and adopts a Saaaarf London 'Cockney' twang. You can tell he's been practising too. I reckon he's gutted not to have been born within the sound of Bow Bells. Keep it up mate, hopefully one day you'll be fluent!

The other thing you realise after chatting to Joe about his goal scoring exploits at the clubs he's played for, is what an impressive record he had.

Unfortunately for Allon, it has been the timing of his transfers that blighted his career, something he admits. Perhaps his choice of clubs after leaving Brentford was suspect too.

As fans, especially in those far off, pre-internet days, it was never clear what was going on behind the scenes and Joe was packed off to Port Vale in a deal that would never see The Bees recoup their investment and before he had the chance to say goodbye to supporters he described as "different class".

Geordie Joe took a fair bit of tracking down but the long train journey to Newcastle and then on to Chester-Le-Street was well worth it. Fantastic company and a natural story teller, it was a pleasure to get the chance to catch up and chat with Joe after all these years, even though his friend's greyhound tips at the race track cost me an arm and a leg.

Wasn't the Anglo Italian [1992-1993] competition just an unwelcome distraction from the league in the end? We did really well but maybe it would have been better in hindsight to have concentrated on picking up league points?

"Yeah for sure. When we beat Derby I thought we could take that into our league form. When we played them on Boxing Day that year, we beat them 2-1 at home, Neil Smillie crossed the ball and one of their players put the ball into his own net and I scored the other. I ran down the wing and beat the 'keeper from the angle.

Just think, Derby had just spent £2.5m on Craig Short, £2m on Gabbiadini, £2m on Kitson, they were like the Fulham of the time spending money like wildfire.

In the Anglo Italian against Derby we got beat 4-3 at home and then beat them 2-1 at the Baseball Ground and got done on the away goals. So it was a confidence booster as we knew the next time we played them we had them in the bag, we knew we should have the beating of them.

But as a distraction, well, it was a chance of getting to Wembley and if we'd got there we would have filled it that year. In the end Derby got stuffed 3-1 by Cremonese.

But it was the league that was our bread and butter. I remember I got a couple of niggles after that and had a bit of a loss of form. I also fell out with Phil Holder too when I was sent off in the reserves.

We were playing in that silly league where you play against the semi-professionals and there was this kid playing for Sutton United who'd been kicking the shit out of me for an hour and a half and as we were coming off of the pitch, I hit him and all hell let loose. Graham Pearce spotted me do it, because I caught

Brentford v Swansea 1993— Joe winds up a defender

him with a fucking belter, and there were complaints from some of the Brentford fuddy-duddies. It was stupid playing a game like that on a Thursday when there was a league match on the Saturday and I had a bust up with Holder and Pearce and there was a little bit of bad feeling.

So Phil put me on the bench for a couple of games and then as the team started going down the league, the crowd started to have a go at some of the players and I remember in one game when I was warming up, somebody had a go at Batesie.

I don't know if you know Jamie, but as a big centre half, he was one of the gentlest kids in the world off the park. It's obvious why he was so placid now though, after the sex allegations in the *News of the World*. Anyway, Jamie heard these fans having a go at him and turned round and told them to fuck off and these three blokes came towards Batesie and I told them to get out the way. Then they said something to me and I offered them out. I guess they just caught us at the wrong time. Supporters are entitled to their own views, but I was getting that het up.

I remember the next game after that incident we were at home to Barnsley and we all knew we just had to win. I came on as sub and within five minutes I scored a goal, I went past Gerry Taggart their centre half and I did my back in and had to come straight off. I think I was only on the pitch about eight minutes. I remember pulling the 'keeper back. I thought it was a foul but the referee didn't give it, so I carried on and lobbed the ball over the 'keeper. That was game over for me though."

Relegation at Bristol City. What Happened Joe?

"Holder left me out at Ashton Gate - he put me on the bench again. I fell out with Phil again before that match. We had to field our strongest team and I honestly went ape-shit about it. I told him to give me the chance and I'd get him out of the shit. I said to Phil that I'd got him out of the shit last week and I'd do it again against Bristol, but he chose to play Bliss [Gary Blissett] with someone else. He turned round to me and said that he thought Blissett and me were too similar and that we couldn't play together.

Yet he was one of my best mates on and off of the park at Brentford and I'll tell you what, for a couple of players who supposedly couldn't play together, we scored about fifty goals between us [Allon's estimate] in the games we played together.

I'd love to see the stats for that, because he had a good season before he went to Wimbledon. I used to get the arsehole when he used to say that about Bliss and me. Who gave a toss at the time how we played as long as we won games?

In our situation then we didn't want to be playing like Brazil, we just wanted to be winning games and we needed goal scorers like me on the pitch.

But at Ashton Gate, at the end of the day, Phil picked the team and he picked the team he thought would save his head, but his head went. I was very disappointed that he got sacked. I phoned him up afterwards and he was fine about it. I considered him a mate, but it showed me that you can't have mates at that level. There's no loyalty in football, it's cut-throat, I tell you.

My goals-per-game record was good and you can't take that away. I was doing the business for Holder, he bought me, but then he stopped playing me in every game. I was gutted he wasn't playing me.

I remember I was training with injuries and he still said my attitude was wrong. All I wanted to do was play. So many times I got Phil out of the shit, like at Wolves away. I scored probably two of my flukiest goals ever in my life, but Molineux was packed that day and Brentford won 2-1, it was a cracking win, Wolves were near the top of the league and my mate Dave Beasant was in goal.

I remember going one-on-one with him, I gave him the eyes, and he just stood still and the ball went past him. I remember thinking 'I can't believe that went in'. We had a great night out after that.

Just look back at the kind of teams we did well against in that division, Derby County, Wolverhampton Wanderers and Sunderland and we murdered all three of them away. If we had the ability to do that we really shouldn't have gone down. We had a cracking side.

Did Holder do enough to turn things around?

"Kenny Samson was already finished when he came to Brentford and Alan Dickens, another mate while I was at Chelsea, wasn't used well by Holder. It was strange. Yes we did have injuries, we missed Terry Evans a lot. He was out with a knee injury and it proved to be a big factor, because when Millie [Keith Millen] was alongside Terry we were a better side. Big Tel was the stopper and Millie used to mop up. But little Billy Manuel did well, he used to get roped in, but then we had those two kids from the Outer Hebrides or wherever [laughs], Luscombe and Chalmers. They came over from the Channel Islands and thought they were Matt Le Tissier, they weren't even Matt Finish let alone Matt Le Tissier! What we really needed was another class midfield player, someone who would command respect.

We did have Detzi Kruyzinksi, but I used to look at him in training and think he used to live on the streets.

Honestly, I used to look at him and think there's no way he can be a player, he was like a fucking tramp. He was a heavy boy as well. He did have ability, obviously, but maybe the discipline side of things was wrong."

Were the players disciplined enough at the time? There seemed to be a big drinking culture and Jamie Bates has even admitted since that he didn't even travel down to Bristol for the relegation decider that season as he decided to go to Southend drinking with his mates that weekend.

"There were a lot of occasions where we did have a good time, yeah, but at the end of the day we used to work our nuts off in training. I've never met a player yet who fucks about before the game, there's plenty of time afterwards. We never had a drink before the game. We always had a couple of pints after training on a Thursday afternoon, but that was forty eight hours before the match.

The good thing about it was there wasn't just two or three of the players who used to go out, there used to be fourteen or fifteen of us. I think as long as you're all pissing in the same pot as it were, all out together, what's wrong with that?

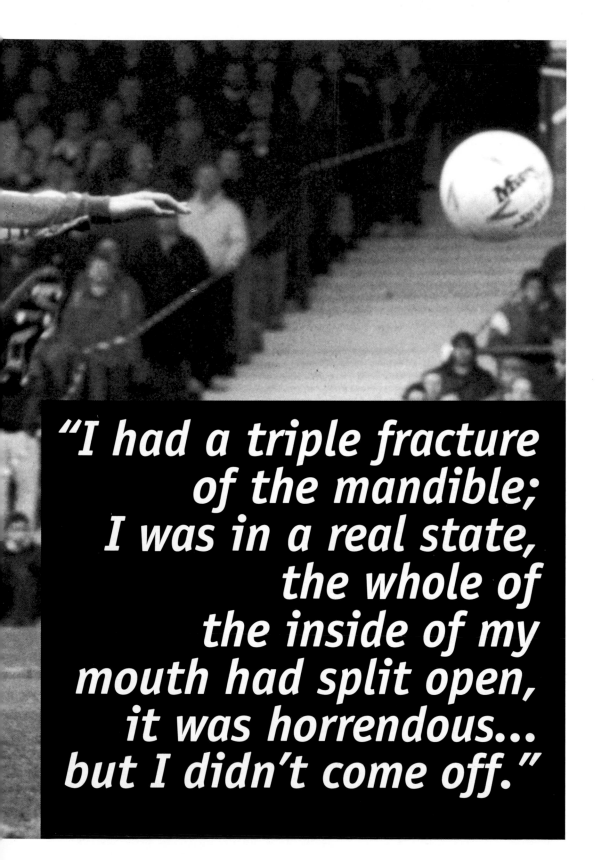

"I had a triple fracture
of the mandible;
I was in a real state,
the whole of
the inside of my
mouth had split open,
it was horrendous...
but I didn't come off."

We were all spread out over London too. I was living out in Hertfordshire, Billy Manuel was out in Eltham, Milly was in Croydon and Terry Evans was in Uxbridge, yet we always used to be out together in Ealing or wherever. That was good I think."

But relegation didn't just sneak up on us in the end. It had been staring us in the face for at least a month. What do you think could have been done to have avoided the drop?

"Play me for a start! At the end of the day I've never been a lot of trouble to any manager I've played for, even Webby the following season, who was one of the biggest disciplinarians in the world. But I would help any kid who was on the park. I would only shout at players I thought deserved being shouted at.

I mean Marcus Gayle used to frustrate the hell out of me, and I've been proved right. He got a kick up the arse and he became a Jamaican international. Now, he had so much ability in his left toe compared to half the others and he was such a lovely kid, but he needed a kick up the arse. I could see there were fortunes for him to make. The crowd must have looked at me and thought 'he's giving Gayle some stick all of the time'.

I used to scream at him to either get a decent cross into the area or win a header, but Marcus was 6ft 3" and couldn't win a header. He used to always be out with us but never used to drink as he was a Born Again Christian. But then again, so was Mickey fucking Bennett and he still gave me that right-hander. The hand of God!"

So talk us through that infamous training session!!

"I never saw it coming! I turned round and then next thing he'd clocked me while I was running. He said he thought I was going to hit him! We were training and I was on the biggest high of my life, it was my birthday. It was the Monday and we were getting two days off. We'd won in the FA Cup at VS Rugby and I'd scored a goal in that big puddle and Webb had decided to give us two days off because the pitch had been so heavy.

Anyway, for some unknown reason Mickey snapped that day and thought I was going to hit him, but I wasn't. We were running along and I had my mouth open and all of a sudden, Smack! He hit me and my jaw broke. But I didn't go off.

I remember telling Billy Manuel to knock the ball to me but my gob was all spurting blood. I had a triple fracture of the mandible. I was in a real state, the whole of the inside of my mouth had split open, it was horrendous. The Gaffer had seen it, obviously, and he sacked Bennett instantly. But that didn't help me because I was on a great run at the time. I'd scored seven goals in six games and eleven up to that stage of the season. I remember I was scoring goals like they were coming out of my ears. I was hungry like the wolf and was working my balls off in training.

Things were going alright, I was on a good run up until getting sent off in the stupid LDV cup. I remember I was on the floor and felt their players standing on me and I threw a punch. It only caught the referee in the knackers! That's my luck. I was surrounded by players and I managed to punch the referee. So I got suspended because of that, but Webb kept putting me back in the team because he knew I would score him goals.

Then there was the problem about wages. Webb wanted me to take a pay cut, but I'd just signed a three year deal the season before. I told him I wasn't going to take a pay cut, so he said I'd have to go out on loan.

Basically he wanted all the lads to drop down to £500 a week. Whether he had the foresight to see how players wages would escalate or he wanted to buy the club, I don't know. So I said, 'Okay, that's not a problem'.

Southend were up near the top at the time under Barry Fry and that was an infamous week I spent there. I said at the time that Barry Fry had the IQ of a flip-flop, but that was an insult to flip-flops all over the world. He was a fucking idiot. I was out for about eleven weeks with the broken jaw and when I was almost fit again Webb asked me to play in a reserve game. He told me not to go in for any headers, played the full ninety minutes and was knackered. I never trained one day, just came back and played in the reserves. He told me that I was going to play at Barnet away the next day, I said 'right, no problems'. It was a crap game and we drew 0-0, but I got through the game.

There were a few taunts of 'there's only one Mickey Bennett' from the Barnet fans, but let's face it, they're out the league, so who's laughing now? The next game was Bristol Rovers away and I scored a hat trick. We beat Rovers 4-1 and I scored three of them, one from the half-way line!"

The incident with Mickey Bennett really blew up and Webb threatened to resign when the Football League ordered the club to reinstate him as a player. What was all that about?
"Well to be honest I was after retribution big style. I'm not kidding you, it nearly got silly. Fortunately it didn't and I haven't got that on my conscience. At the end of the day I only broke my jaw and jaws mend. I've never ever come across him again, I've never seen him from that day. I'd like to tell you what Vinny Jones said to me in hospital that night when I had all my jaw wired up, but I'd better be careful what I say."

Did you get on with David Webb?
"When he joined he got his secretary to ring me up, and I told her I'd had a few problems with my fitness and that as far as I was concerned the club had done nothing about it. He said he wanted me back, so I said 'right, I'll come back' and we worked on my fitness. I went to see an osteopath in Sutton, a bloke called Johnson, who was looking after the Great Britain athletics team. His son Gary was at Cambridge United at the time.

Anyway, he sorted me out, the alignment of my pelvis and groin was out and I was getting pain all the time. I had a lot of respect for Webb for that, big respect.

I think deep down he liked me, it was a pure financial thing and a business decision. When I went to Port Vale he arranged a deal which meant Brentford got £2,000 every time I played and £1,000 every time I scored.

My debut was Port Vale against Fulham, it was just after dead-line day with four games to go until the end of the season. It ended Port Vale 2 Fulham 0, Joe Allon scored two. So that cost Port Vale £6,000 for that game. Now that's not bad because I thought that's what they wanted me to do. We had another game on the Monday as it was over the Easter Bank Holiday and we were playing at Leyton Orient but I tore my ankle ligaments after five minutes. Another clumsy oaf of a centre half done my ankle and I never played again that season.

At the start of the next season I kept finding myself on the bench all the time, so I said to John Rudge 'what's happening?'. He told me the Chairman had been moaning that I was costing them too much money. I scored ten goals in twelve substitute appearances so it was costing them. But their Chairman didn't like it which wasn't on because they'd got me for nothing but Brentford had paid almost £300,000 for me. So there was a sharp fall out, but I persevered until it came to deadline day the following year. Falkirk came in for me and offered £100,000, so I got my contract out and noticed that Port Vale had dropped the biggest cock-up I'd ever seen on a contract. When I signed, I'd got my signing on fee, but the secretary had mis-typed the year. Port Vale thought they'd signed me for two seasons but because of the cock-up I was a free agent.

So instead of signing for Falkirk I told them to save their £100,000 and come back and see me at the end of the season. Port Vale wanted me to re-sign a contract on deadline day. I remember we had Portsmouth on the Tuesday night and Vale needed a win to stay up. I scored the goal and we won 1-0, so I was a hero.

Then on the Thursday John Rudge phoned me up and I got my missus to tell him I'd gone fishing. So I went down the pub with the lads. I pointed out the contract mistake to the manager at five minutes past five on deadline day and they couldn't do anything about it. He said to me 'you're a shrewd bastard', and I just went 'Aye, I am!' Vale offered me another deal but I turned them down because they'd messed me about and then I heard that Webby wanted me back.

I told him that I would come back, I loved it at Brentford. He phoned me three times and I told him I'd come back to London, but it never materialised in the end.

I was in a good position financially to organise my next contract. A lot of the players were shit scared of Webb though, I

Allon at the greyhound stadium

wasn't, the only time I did get frightened was when one of the Kray Twins died and there he was on the front page of *The Sun* newspaper carrying the coffin!"

What are the comparisons between Webb and Holder?

"Phil Holder liked to play the Tottenham way. It was the way he'd been brought up. At times I thought that we over played, whereas Webb was more direct. He used to like players to get back behind the ball when we didn't have it."

But it was Holder who had the tag of being the long-ball merchant. Do you think that wasn't strictly true then?

"No. A lot of the time when the long ball was used it was when our options were limited. Graham Benstead used to get the ball and hump it as hard as he could, but all Phil would ever do in training would be pass and move and little five-a-sides. Probably tactically he wasn't as good as Webb, but it's about having the players who do the job, which brings me back to the likes of Luscombe and Chalmers."

Not forgetting Murray Jones either. Was he as awful on the training pitch as he was on the football pitch?

"He was rubbish. A really nice guy, but rubbish. I think he only ever scored one goal in training ever. I think Holder liked him because he was part of the South London connection. He was big friends with Keith Millen too. I didn't know who he was for the first three months I was there, I couldn't believe somebody actually paid money for him. He was a big lad but he was like a gentle giant as well. Nobody really used to bother him as he was normally down the stiffs end of the training ground. I remember Phil throwing him a shirt in training when Holder was trying to have a go at me and I thought Murray had cum in his pants!"

Joe is currently working for local radio as a football pundit on Saturday afternoons and for Newcastle United as part of their match day hospitality team.

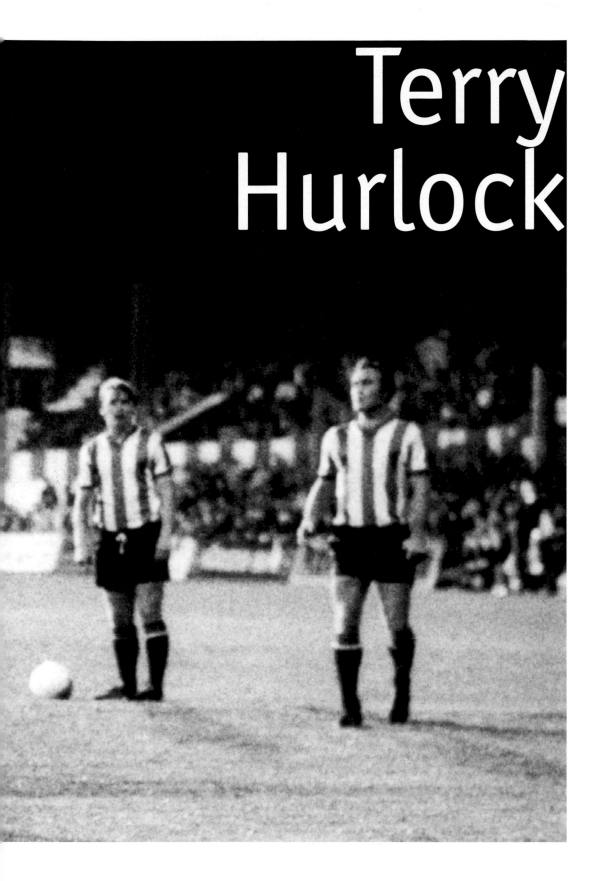

Terry Hurlock

Date: Thursday 13th June, 2002
Venue: Terry's house, Loughton, Essex
Era: 1980-1986 Appearances: 263 Goals: 24

What you see is certainly what you get with Terry Hurlock, both on and off of the football pitch. After meeting the man, I can honestly say that every preconception I had from my days watching Terry from the Griffin Park terraces proved correct.

As a player at Brentford in the early eighties, a raw and unkempt looking twenty-two-year-old took the Third Division by storm within weeks. Hurlock would cement a reputation as an talented, uncompromising midfielder with a string of outstanding performances and crunching tackles.

Terry was a hard man, but there was more to his game than that. He was a leader and I can never remember him being malicious. To Bees fans he was always firm but fair, but then again, we would say that - he was on our side back then.

Hurlock was Brentford through and through while he was at Griffin Park - Terry spent longer at Brentford than at any other club in his career - he lived next to the ground and never gave anything less than 100 per cent in his red and white shirt. Terry is a true cult Brentford legend in every sense of the word.

The portrait on his living room wall, showing Hurlock in his England 'B' shirt, and the *Evening Standard* Player of the Month trophy from his Millwall days, unfortunately point to the fact that his best memories in the game were away from Griffin Park. But after chatting to Terry, it's clear he has very fond memories of his time in west London and holds Brentford Football Club and the local people in high regard.

Surprisingly though, there is no millionaire ex-footballer lifestyle for Terry despite some lucrative years at Glasgow Rangers and in the top flight with Millwall and Southampton - Hurlock lives in an unpretentious, modest home on a Loughton estate.

I got the impression that Terry didn't really take it all in while he was involved in football and that he just played his game, got changed, then got back to enjoying himself down the pub with the lads. Hopefully when the club gets round to finding a suitable new home they'll include a permanent Brentford museum and Hurlock will be able to take his rightful place in the Brentford Hall of Fame.

Were there any other clubs in for you at the time Fred Callaghan spotted you at Leytonstone?

"I heard that Dave Webb was having a look at me while he was at Bournemouth. But the day Webby came down to see me play I was injured so I missed out. I was happy that I got the opportunity to come to Brentford as I thought I'd missed my chance.

I left school and didn't have any qualifications and was doing a bit of this and that - nothing kind of jobs really - and I didn't know where I was going.

I was with West Ham as a kid but they released me at eighteen and I went and played with Enfield for a bit when they were the top non-league side.

While I was at Leytonstone David Crown got picked up by Brentford a little while before me and that did my head in. I was gutted it wasn't me. I never thought I'd get my chance."

Fred obviously had a lot of faith in your ability as you went pretty much straight into the starting line-up.

"Fred was great and I looked up to him while he was there. In fact I've never caused any of my managers any bother and have learned something from all of them really. It helped having players like Chris Kamara and Stan Bowles alongside me in midfield though.

Stan would be spraying lovely balls about the pitch; Kamara would be running all over the place tackling with his long legs... I dunno what the fuck I was doing? [Laughs] Getting booked I suppose!

Bowlesie took me under his wing and showed me the inside of virtually every betting shop and pub in West London. He knew some right shady characters round Shepherds Bush and we used to knock about with a right wrong crowd.

I still see Stan quite a bit and he has been staying with me for

2002— Hurlock beside his England 'B' portrait

the past couple of weekends. In fact most of the boys knew how to have a good drink. It was different back then though, it's not the same now, but it was okay to go down the pub with the lads after training for a few pints back then."

Do you remember anything about your debut in Brentford's win at Fellows Park, Walsall?

"Well I remember that on the way up there on the coach Fred made the driver pull over, gave me 50p, then told me to go and buy some socks. I never had any socks on and for some reason he thought I should be wearing some.

The game was on the telly I think as I did have it on video at some stage but I've lost it along the way. I'd love to get hold of that again as none of my kids have really seen me in action back then and it'd be nice to show them their old dad in action."

Callaghan's sides always seemed to have solid midfields and exciting strikers but the defence always let him down. Would it be fair to say that Danis Salman was the only really decent defender at the club while you were there?

"Danis was a good player yeah. His speed would get him out of a lot of problems. I think you might be right though, maybe Fred lacked some experience in sorting out defences.

We never had many problems scoring goals though with Francis Joseph and Tony Mahoney in the side.

Joseph was a good player and he used to frighten a lot of defences to death and boy could be drink too. Francis and me used to get on well. Gary Roberts too, he was another good lad."

Fred's teams always seemed to have a lot of skilled individuals but he seemed to have a lot of trouble moulding them into a successful team didn't he?

"To be honest I never thought about it much. I never thought much about football tactics and that and I never looked at what Fred should or shouldn't be doing to be honest. I just got out there and did what I did."

2002– Terry's house during the World Cup

"My house was right next to Griffin Park. I used to live and drink with everyone round there and loved my time at the club and living in the town."

Your whole-hearted style of play brought you attention from plenty of referees - but did you think you deserved it?

"I don't think I could have played in this day and age at all, I'd miss about twenty games a season these days. You can't be physical at all now."

Martin Lange was a young Chairman at the time you joined. Did he have much to do with you?

"Lange was as good as gold to me and he got me out of a lot of scrapes outside football for doing this and that. I've got a lot of time for Lange and he made me buy a house in Brentford. I would never have thought about buying my own place back then and I owe him for making me buy something with my money."

Did you foresee the potential of your career back then? Obviously you went on to play at the very top in British football but when did you first realise that you had what it took to really go places in the game?

"I think when I started getting the Man of the Match award regularly. Eventually I thought, 'hold on a minute, I can't be that bad you know...' I never had an agent or anything, they weren't really that big back then, but I should have done really I suppose. I wasn't really clued up on that side of things."

Frank McLintock and John Docherty eventually replaced Fred Callaghan - Docherty would subsequently help you get to the First Division with Millwall.

"Yeah I got on well with Doc. Everyone was petrified of him though. He used to be all quiet and then go fucking mad at the players and everyone was always looking over their shoulders making sure he wasn't around. He was always shouting at me 'get on those scales you fat bastard, show me how much you weigh this week...'

Frank was different to Fred though, he was just like one of us. Docherty sorted me out a good move to Millwall after I went to Reading though. I still get a lot of calls from Millwall and I go over there from time to time."

When I watch Frank McLintock on the telly today I often say to myself, "yeah, you can talk a good game Frank, but you were never good enough to get Brentford out of Division Three were you?" Why do you think Frank failed to succeed at Brentford? Was it lack of money?

"I dunno anything about what financial stuff he had to deal with, I never thought about if there was money for players and that, but maybe Frank got found out a bit."

Do you remember Rowan Alexander? He was the first 'somersaulting goal-scorer' to be seen at Griffin Park I think.

"God, yeah, I remember him. He was a little bloke but he didn't half have a spring on him and he could get up for a lot of headers."

Do you remember much about the Freight Rover cup run? It may have ended in disappointment but Wembley was great.

"I don't remember much about the run, but I remember the final itself at Wembley. All the boys had been away on holiday together and we got back a week before the game. Looking back it wasn't a very clever thing to do for the club to send us all away before and we all came back fucking knackered.

I remember it all nearly went off with another football team [Port Vale] while we were away, I'm not saying who the team was, but all our lads were right up for giving them a good kicking. One of their players had said something to Gary Roberts, which wasn't surprising really as he was always winding somebody or another up the wrong way after a drink. [Laughs] I can't believe he's a copper now.

Anyway, luckily somebody talked us all out of it because it would have been a very regrettable incident. I definitely remember that everyone wanted it though. We arrived back in England at 4am on the Saturday morning. I was getting married later the same day and I had to be at the service at 10am.

The crowd and the atmosphere at Wembley was amazing though, I don't remember an awful lot about the game but I know I didn't play well. There was something wrong with me and

I didn't know what, my legs were completely dead and I struggled to get through the game."

Reading took the league by storm the year you left Brentford. You moved with about a quarter of the season to go, but were there any other clubs in for you?

"Not that anyone told me about. Ian Porterfield and Reading was the only deal I heard about, but I thought it was a good move for me to go down there at the time."

Do you think you were worth more than £92,000? It didn't seem very much money for someone with your potential.

"I never thought about that. I have never been one to think I was worth this or worth that. As I said, maybe I should have done but at the time I never really thought about it.

Porterfield tried to make me move down and live in Reading but I never wanted to. It only took me thirty-five minutes each way so I never saw the point, but I remember I used to love getting back to Brentford. Porterfield wasn't happy with that at all and we fell out a bit over it, so when John Docherty came in for me with Millwall I jumped at the chance."

What is your best memory of being at Brentford?

"Just the people and living around the ground really. My house was right next to Griffin Park. I used to live and drink with everyone round there and loved my time at the club and living in the town."

Who was the best player while you were at the club?

"I'd have to say Chris Kamara - he was a very good player. Gary Roberts came close though - he was a very skillful winger."

With you and Kamara in the side there couldn't have been many players who'd try their luck, but can you remember any opponents who would try and give you a tough time?

"Not many, although I remember Portsmouth's Mick Tait always had a bit of a go."

Unfortunately Brentford were the opponents in the 'friendly' where you broke a leg and effectively finished your career?

"Yeah that little **** Martin Grainger went in high on me and busted my leg. There was only a week to go before the start of the season and I pulled back from going in hard, everyone does with just a week to go, but Grainger went over the top of the ball.

I've heard since that he's got a habit of doing things like that and people say that he has got a right nasty streak. A lot of people since have told me exactly what they think he is like and if I ever found out that he meant to do it - I dread to think - I'd want to strangle him I reckon."

So you won't exactly be cheering Birmingham City on in the Premier League next season?

"No I won't, no way! There's nothing wrong with going in hard, football is a physical game, but if a player intentionally tries to injure another player badly to prove something then that is well out of order.

The only other time I was in so much pain during a game was away at Wigan with Brentford. Wigan were always a tough team to play against back then and we never had much joy with them. I remember another late tackle coming in and I did my ligaments which kept me out for quite a while."

Do you still get some jip from the injury?

"Yeah I do, in fact I get jip from both my knees too. But I'm off the booze at the moment, which is hard during the World Cup believe me. I'm trying to get a bit fitter again."

1972— Nelmes [second from right] celebrates promotion with the team

Alan Nelmes

Date: Tuesday 28th May, 2002
Venue: Middleton-on-Sea, West Sussex
Era: 1967-1976 Appearances: 350 Goals: 2

Brentford Football Club owed as much to the efforts of its loyal players as it did to the tireless work from supporters' groups when turning imminent extinction into survival following the traumatic events of 1967 when QPR tried to kill the club.

Brentford Football Club was on its knees, and even though the threat of takeover was eventually removed, harsh financial constraints meant the club was barely able to field a team.

At one stage there were only twelve players on the books, so it was a relief that there was no obligation to name more than one substitute back then, otherwise we may have had to ask for volunteers from the crowd.

A lot was expected of those who were chosen to pull on the red and white stripes during that traumatic era and Jimmy Sirrel's troops needed to be versatile, fit and resilient. It was left to players like Tommy Higginson, Gordon Phillips, Alan Hawley, Peter Gelson and Alan Nelmes to lead by example.

Later, under Frank Blunstone, these solid, dependable workhorses were joined by the likes of John O'Mara and Stewart Houston, who, combined with an attractive flowing style of play, brought the crowds flooding back through the turnstiles and achieved promotion from the basement division.

We tracked down one of the most consistent and reliable players from this era, Alan Nelmes, and drove down to Middleton-on-Sea in Sussex for a long chat about his time at the club. Nelmes has hardly changed either. He may not work out on the training pitch every day, but twenty five years after hanging up his boots, the Bees stalwart is still as fit as a fiddle. Nelmes plays tennis most days and weighs less now than he did when he was a professional.

You joined the club during one of the most disturbing eras in Brentford's history. Can you describe the situation the club was in from a player's perspective?

"As players we couldn't let it get to us. We had an incredibly close team spirit at the time, which was essential. I'd joined the club from Chelsea where it was very much a case of them and us and the contrast at Brentford was incredible. We were all in it together and because we had such a small squad we all became very close.

Jimmy Sirrel, who was the manager at the time, was a good boss. He knew how to get the best out of his players and even doubled up as the club's physio and treated all of the squad.

But the players we had at Brentford were expected to be versatile which showed in how many positions I played in. I even played up front as a centre forward in a game at Notts County and I actually scored."

Did the club's off the pitch gloom affect morale in the dressing room?

"No not really, not as I remember. I think the worst of the troubles were behind us when I joined, but as I say, there was a tremendous team spirit and as players you just have to get on with it. After being stuck in the reserves at Chelsea and having to train in a completely separate training ground from Tommy Docherty and the first-teamers, I was really happy to be playing every week."

Between the start of the 1968-69 season and the end of 1971-72, you missed just three games including two consecutive seasons where you didn't miss a single match. You made your 100th consecutive appearance away at Aldershot in a 2-1 win. It must have been a very proud day for you?

"Yes, I was very proud of that record. As a professional footballer you want to reach a level of consistency where you command a regular place in the team and that is what happened. I think I'd reached the age where I was at the peak of my strength and fitness and I felt at my best between those years.

I'd always enjoyed my days at Brentford and anything I achieved with the club, especially the year when I won the Players' Player of the Year Trophy - that was a big thing for me. To be

2002— Alan proves he hasn't lost his touch

voted the best player of the season by your fellow professionals was superb and I took that as a real compliment. To gain promotion and win that at the same time was superb."

You saw both highs and lows in the FA Cup at Brentford, 1967 saw humiliation against Southern League Guildford City, 1971 saw elation from a great cup run. Do you remember much about our defeat at Joseph's Road, Guildford?
"Actually, not a lot to be honest. I think over the years the bad memories just fade away and you only really remember the good times vividly."

I bet your memories of the 1971 Cup run are a lot less fuzzy. Do you recall much about that year's clashes?
"Yes, especially the games at Cardiff and Hull City, they were really memorable. We went down to Cardiff by train and stayed in a really nice hotel in the hills overlooking the city. The atmosphere in the ground was fantastic. You really couldn't hear your team-mates calling with 23,000 fans shouting. There was noise all around us, it was a very intimidating atmosphere to be playing in. It was a great win for the players and we had a few drinks that night. The game at Hull was just as noisy, there was just under 30,000 people there. We were unlucky to lose at Hull, Bobby Ross gave us the lead but we couldn't hang on. I am sure, to this day, that our 'keeper Gordon Phillips was fouled for their equaliser."

The Cup run seemed to lift the club's fortunes and hopes were high ahead of the new season in the summer of 1971. It turned out to be a memorable year and just what the club needed following the 1967 crisis.
"The previous season's cup run was instrumental in the success that season I think. It gave us the extra confidence we needed as players and we were able to use our good experiences in the FA Cup to help us sustain a decent promotion challenge. The Cup run definitely gave us the lift we needed and we were much stronger because of our achievements the previous year."

"There were 18,000 Brentford fans and we won with a John O'Mara goal, it must have been the biggest crowd I had played in front of at Griffin Park."

John O'Mara was added to the team too. His arrival from Wimbledon made a big difference didn't it?

"John was a big man, about 6ft 5" and very quick. I remember I'd had a run in with him in a reserve game while he was at Wimbledon. This long ball was played up into our area and as I jumped to clear it, Wallop!, I felt this punch in my back and it flattened me.

Anyway, Jimmy Sirrel had always told us that whenever a late tackle came in, not to retaliate straight away, we should just bide our time and get the return in later in the game.

So that's what I did. In the second half this ball was played in again and I clattered him. When he joined Brentford we both had respect for each other straight away and we really got on well. He was a very good player then. He was at his peak. It's a shame that he was sold, I know the club had offers for him, but they wanted to keep him, but he eventually went to Blackburn the following season which was maybe a little bit too late for John to go on to the top.

Maybe he waited a little bit too long for that move because things didn't work out well at Rovers. Obviously it was a shame for him but good for us because we kept him at the club longer.

It just shows you, if you're getting good service and the pattern of play and players in the team suit you, then to move on isn't always in your best interests. Sometimes it's better to stay where you are."

The tactics that Frank Blunstone used were obviously popular with the squad. It was good attacking football.

"You're right, the players were really comfortable with what was expected of us and I think it showed in the way we played. We had a lot of respect for Frank. He had a network of scouts all over the country that used to keep tabs on our opponents and report back to him.

So before a game he would roughly know what to expect for our opponents. He would be out every night of the week watching games, studying other players and teams. He was an extremely knowledgeable manager."

O'Mara was infamous for his physical style and retaliation. At the tail end of the promotion season he was handed a five match disciplinary ban by the Football League for the bookings he'd received. That must have seemed very harsh at the time and could have affected the promotion push?

"His physical presence was one of his main attributes and he used to get in there where it hurt. If you play like that, then obviously there's a little bit of niggle that goes on. It's a bit like Alan Smith at Leeds now - he can take it and give it at the same time. But we could throw those crosses in knowing that John would get on the end of them. It was a harsh punishment though, I think they thought they had to curb John."

How about you Alan, were you ever sent off?

"No never, I received a few yellows but never a red. I suppose my mentor was Jimmy Sirrel really and as I said, he used to tell the players to wait their time and do it sensibly. Obviously we used to go in with a few late ones and get booked for it, but basically if you're sensible and go for a 50-50 you can get away with things if you play honestly.

I was quite a physical player, I used to think that as a defender the opponent would have to know that I was there and think twice about taking the ball as they knew I'd be coming in behind them. I found that good players would go in regardless.

Players at the time, like Phil Boyer, Ted McDougall, Billy Jennings at Watford, people like that, they would carry on whatever the situation. Even if you'd hit them a couple of times in 50-50s, they'd still go in there where it hurt. They got their head in where the boots were flying. They were good players."

It was about the time of O'Mara's enforced absence that Stewart Houston arrived from Chelsea. What did he add to the Brentford team?

"He was very good. He started off playing out of position though, playing up front. At Chelsea I'd always known him as a defender and yet he played up front and really did play well there for us. When he moved on to Manchester United he was always left-back and yet at Brentford, he was played as a striker. He was superb. He was quick and strong and he gave us a good outlet. When we used to go to away matches, a lot of times you would basically defend, but you'd give it to him and he used to go on the outside and hold the ball up superbly for us. Having a player like that, who was so good yet was able to play in such a lot of positions, was a tremendous asset. Stewart obviously matured much more when he went to Manchester United."

Was Houston the best player while you were at the club?
"Yes I think so, but Roger Cross was always good, always impressive. He would hold the ball up, shield it well, then lay it off. He did a very good job for us."

As we closed in on promotion there were a few jitters and Brentford went down at bottom of the table Crewe Alexandra. What did the manager say to the players after that defeat... Did he tear you off a strip?
"Well, he was very disappointed, but that's how seasons go sometimes. There are always fixtures that you should win but somehow don't. Whether we were just getting a bit tense in the run-in and thinking that we were nearly there, we just didn't perform as we should have done."

Are there any games from that 1971-72 promotion season that really stand out for you?
"Yes, Crewe at home on Boxing Day that year. There were 18,000 Brentford fans at Griffin Park and we won with a John O'Mara goal, it must have been the biggest crowd I had played in front of at Griffin Park. The other match I clearly remember was against Exeter in the final home game of the season where we knew we had to win to go up.

The pressure Bobby Ross was under when he stepped up to score from the penalty spot must have been unbelievable. It was a tight match, and Exeter upped their game for the big crowd at Brentford [14,000]. They played pretty well that day, but to hear the final whistle and the roar of the crowd was tremendous.

1970– Nelmes during an ever-present season

To get out of that league was such a relief but it was such a shame to achieve that and then see the team not strengthened properly. I mean, we got David Court and David Jenkins - both were on frees and both had seen better days. They were the only additions to the squad really. Just a couple more players to give us some strength in depth would have given us a chance of staying up in the old Third Division. It was such a waste, there was no foresight."

The promotion celebrations after the Exeter game must have been good. There were players who were in that side that had been with you for a number of years, players like Jackie Graham, Peter Gelson, Bobby Ross. There must have been a good party?

"Yes there was. We had a few parties in some of the players' houses - some of the lads really liked to entertain... Not naming any names."

There were a few party animals in the camp were there?

"One or two yes, especially one of those from 'Scottish origins' shall we say! You didn't really want to get too close to him at training on a Monday morning, as you could smell the weekend being sweated away!"

You've mentioned your feeling of disappointment that following promotion the Board didn't bringing in stronger players. Was there a feeling in the squad that you had been let down and that there was a lack of ambition at the club?

"Yes, there was. To bring in two players that were simply not up to the job was a blow. It was surprising, because David Jenkins had moved from Arsenal to Tottenham for about £100,000, which was an awful lot of money at the time.

But at Brentford he just didn't do a thing for us. He didn't look capable of doing a job, he hardly played for us and when he did, well, he was very poor.

It was a let down to feel that they didn't have that ambition there, which I suppose has carried on through the years at Brentford, hasn't it? With that little bit of foresight and capitalising on our good season things could have been very different at Brentford today.

But you saw the same happen this [2001-02] season. The club could have really gone forward."

There was a quote in the Middlesex Chronicle at the time, which said: "Since the 1967 episode I am afraid the club has become very small minded. Admittedly that was necessary for a couple of years or so, but timidity of this sort prompts me to believe that promotion last year was an unwelcome accident, which has now been rectified." As a player at the heart of the squad, was that a fair reflection?

"I think that was about spot on. To end up back at square one, after battling so hard was most disappointing, it really was.

We trained hard all week, got the results, we had a good manager and the basis of a good squad, so we felt we could have done well in the Third Division. We only needed two or three other players to come in and bolster the squad."

The board couldn't have been worried about finances quite as much either. We'd averaged almost 12,000 at home during the 1971-72 promotion season with a wafer thin squad. In hindsight there were few excuses for them not to have backed their manager better.

"Blimey, was the average crowd as high as that? What would they give for those kind of gates at Brentford now?"

Frank Blunstone resigned after relegation the next season, claiming he was never allowed to manage as he would have liked. Were the players gutted to see him go?

"Yes we were. Especially when Mike Everitt came in. He was such a different manager. He didn't have the technical expertise that Frank had got and you felt as if the club wasn't going anywhere with him. It was such a let down, it really was. It definitely affected morale and there wasn't a good reaction from the players to his arrival."

2002— Alan enjoying an active retirement in Sussex

So was Everitt bad news all round from your point of view?

"Yes he was. He just didn't seem to have any knowledge of the game. It was a shame because Frank was very advanced in his thinking, ahead of his time really. Very good tactically and it was a step backwards to have Mike."

Did these managerial developments make you question whether or not you wanted to remain at the club?

"Yes it was tragic, you felt so sorry, you could see it all crumbling. I went on the transfer list just after Everitt arrived and a couple of clubs came in for me, but I didn't really have the heart to go anywhere else. I wanted to stay with the club and eventually I thought 'although he's here... I'll give it a go again', and I got back into the side and started playing again.

I knew Everitt wouldn't last, which he didn't. Then John Docherty, my old Brentford team mate, took over."

Was that weird, having a good friend and team mate take over as manager and start calling the shots?

"Yes it was really, although John had a good knowledge of the game and was always going to be a good manager. I'd always got on well with him so I was happy with that. He'd always had a bit to do with coaching and training so it was easy to slot in with him changing roles."

Were you happy to play out your days at Brentford?

"Yes I was, I'd enjoyed it so much. I was nearing the end of my career when John Docherty took over and it was clear that Danis Salman was going to be the future and I didn't want to be just hanging on in there.

I don't have any regrets, as I never really wanted to leave Brentford, but I would have perhaps liked to have had the chance of testing myself at a higher level.

I mean, we went to Manchester United in the League Cup in 1975 and we lost 2-1 after going one up again. I had a blinder up there against Sammy McIlroy, then you think, 'could I have done that week in, week out?'.

I really remember that game well. Keith Lawrence scored with a lovely header and Bill Glazier was in goal for us. With about twenty minutes to go there was a bit of drizzle and we gave a free kick away just outside the area. Macari took it but miss-kicked the ball. Bill Glazier, with all his experience, went down and let it slip through his hands and let them back in the game. McIlroy scored again about ten minutes later and we lost 2-1.

It just annoys you that Bill, at the end of his career, didn't really have his heart in the club or the game and you think, 'why didn't he just retire gracefully before he got to the club?'

There were about 25,000 at Old Trafford and the atmosphere was really good - to play in front of them week in week out can only be good for your game can't it?"

You were given a good testimonial against Chelsea. It was a cracking crowd wasn't it?

"Well I was really lucky. For some reason we couldn't fit the fixture in anywhere so it was eventually played two years after I'd left. Chelsea had been down from the top flight, then got promoted again that year, and Brentford went up the same season.

By the time the testimonial came around I remember we had a couple of really grotty weeks weather-wise and there hadn't been much football played. I remember I'd been given a good plug on the TV by Saint and Greavesie and there was a bumper crowd of nearly 10,000. For a testimonial it was an excellent crowd.

It was a very proud day plus I got a nice cheque. But it was ironic, I'd gone through my whole playing career without any real injuries, then I got a cartilage injury before my testimonial."

Were you awarded the obligatory 'last minute penalty' during your testimonial match?

"[Laughs] No I wasn't, not like they do now! Even Matt Le Tissier's son was allowed to score a penalty during his dad's testimonial at Southampton last season."

How about the money back then. Did you consider that you earned an above average salary?

"No, not at all. I think the money we were paid at the time was very average. In fact I think the money I earn on security at Gatwick Airport now is about the same with inflation. We didn't earn that much at all. I think our win bonus was only about £4. Maybe Roger Cross and Stewart Houston were on a bit more when they were brought in, but I think everyone else in the squad was on a par as far as wages were concerned."

At that stage had you really prepared for not being a footballer any more, emotionally, physically and financially? It must be quite a daunting prospect?

"Well, I was quite lucky that my mum and dad had an off licence business on the south coast which they'd been running for a few years, so I always had that at the back of my mind. But saying that, it still leaves a massive void in your life.

For so long you've been aiming for a career as a footballer, then to actually achieve your dream is fantastic. I had worked so hard to get there and enjoyed every minute of it, to actually then be leaving the game was a big thing.

When you'd been working towards a game on a Saturday all week and you didn't have that any more, it takes quite a few years to get used to that. But I thought, well, I hadn't got that big a name away from Brentford and coaches and managers all get the sack after a couple of years, and was I just putting off the inevitable by trying to stay in the game?

With my mum and dad working in shops all their lives, moving around quite a lot, I felt my education had suffered, so I thought I should move somewhere and get established so my sons could get a good education.

So I moved down to the south coast. But retiring from football still left a big hole in my life."

You were also in the side where that infamous dog ran onto the pitch and attacked Chic Brodie in the Brentford goal. What do you remember about that afternoon?

"Oh the dog! I've seen the clip they always show on the TV since and as the ball was played past me the dog hurtled after it and hit Chic's knee. It was quite a big dog, quite some size and that put his ligaments out and he was given a free transfer at the end of the season. The dog basically ended his Brentford career.

It looked comical but there was a very serious side too. Chic had a bad incident with a garden fork as well. He was due to play on the Saturday and he'd been doing a bit of gardening on the Friday afternoon and ended up putting a fork through his foot.

I suppose he had a bit of clay to get through and gave it a good 'whack', and the fork went straight through his foot. Dave Simmons was another player who had a bad injury around then. He was in a hotel, just chatting and walking along, when he went straight through a plate glass door. It shattered and it was a really serious injury, in fact he nearly died as the glass severed an artery in his arm just above the wrist. It was very nasty."

What's your best memory of your time at Brentford?
"I think it was picking up the Players' Player of the Season Trophy. Obviously promotion was important, but that award was my biggest moment really. I felt so proud to have got to a professional club where I felt at home and received Players' Player. To earn their respect was great."

The fans were very fond of you too weren't they?
"I think I won them over in the end. When I first went there I was a utility player and was pushed from pillar to post because the club only had twelve players. Wherever there was an injury they used to put me and that was a bit unsettling - I didn't really get any rhythm. I always used to do my best, but obviously when you're playing in a new position it's difficult."

You finished your Brentford career on a nice round 350 appearances. You were a great servant to the club.
"Yes, including cup games it was spot on 350. Apart from getting married and having my two boys that achievement is the biggest thing to happen in my life. It's just a shame we didn't get any medals for the promotion season, only the Champions got them back then. After you've retired and are sitting at home

watching the telly, it'd be nice to have a few reminders sitting there on the mantlepiece."

What was your goal record like in those games?

"I scored two and I remember them both very vividly! [Laughs] I remember scoring one against Scunthorpe when Kevin Keegan was marking me, I was playing in midfield and I lost Keegan at this corner. I came in and a melee of players went to the near post and the ball came through them and fell to me so I knocked it in. Kevin was just ball watching and I came in behind him. Of course he was only sixteen at the time."

What do you remember of Griffin Park itself? With all the talk of moving away, what springs back into your mind after all these years?

"The dressing room I think. The old one before it burnt down. Just past the brick wall in the forecourt on the right. There was a great big bath in there with massive taps and they used to fill it up with water and then pump steam into it, which was really something else. If the thing was working it was great after a game. It was a little bit different from places like Workington and Barrow I can tell you!

I remember after a game at Workington you had limited time to get the last train back to Carlisle, and when you'd beaten them in the Third Round of the FA Cup like we did, you'd get a freezing cold bath too. If they couldn't beat you on the pitch they'd beat you in the dressing room.

We spent quite a lot of time at the ground as we used to train on Griffin Park as well as play there. Sometimes we used to go over to Gunnesbury Park or an indoor hall for five-a-side, but basically the pitch became a diamond of mud.

I try to get back to Griffin Park two or three times a year, so I've managed to keep up to date with most of the changes at the club over the seasons and I definitely class myself a supporter of the club along with both my sons."

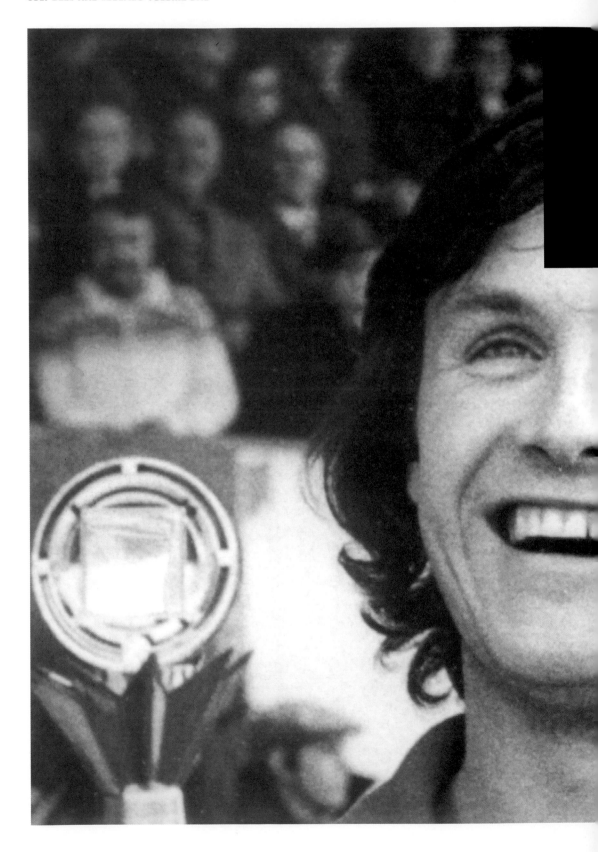

Doug
Allder

Date: Friday 24th May, 2002
Venue: The Park Restaurant, Teddington
Era: 1977-1980 Appearances: 95 Goals: 3

Doug Allder was a real London club man, never leaving the capital as a professional. After serving his apprenticeship at Cold Blow Lane under Millwall boss Benny Fenton, Allder went on to play over 200 games for The Lions before moving to Leyton Orient.

Three years later, after a brief loan spell with Graham Taylor at Watford, Allder made his way to Brentford and completed a unique north, east, south and west London football club circle.

The Bees were well placed in the league when Allder joined in the winter of 1977, but Bill Dodgin wanted more width in his side and better delivery for Andy McCulloch and Steve Phillips up front, so Allder was brought in to play on the left wing.

Allder may have only been at the club for three seasons, but his memories at Brentford under Bill Dodgin and Chairman Dan Tana give a fascinating insight into what was an exciting, flamboyant era at the club.

There was a great expectancy at Griffin Park following promotion to the Third Division and the team were still attracting very healthy crowds. Flowing football, goals-a-plenty, plus the vast and vociferous Royal Oak terrace were the ingredients many thirty-something Bees fans remember - Allder's was the era that got them hooked on Brentford Football Club.

There's no way this first volume of Cult Bees and Legends would have been complete without asking Allder about his legendary toe-to-toe scrap with Sheffield United's Mickey Speight back in 1978 - so it was great to be able to get another piece of Brentford terrace folklore cleared up straight from the horse's mouth and find out what really went on that eventful night.

The brawl has been described as 'the best bust-up ever witnessed on Griffin Park's hallowed turf' - but unfortunately for the Bees player involved the fight remains his biggest legacy in the memories of the majority of Bees fans.

So how did your move to Brentford come about?

"Well it was strange, I'd moved from Millwall to Leyton Orient and things didn't really work out there for me. Then I got a couple of phone calls, one was from Bill Dodgin at Brentford and the other was from Graham Taylor at Watford.

Bill was saying, 'you must come to us, you must come to us', and Graham Taylor came back to me and said pretty much the same. Graham Taylor was struggling with injuries, so I decided to go there for the month.

I played in the first game and we won away the day after I joined. I met Elton John on Watford Junction station the morning of the game and we travelled up to Rochdale together.

Obviously I knew who he was, but I didn't think he'd recognise me. I remember walking past the buffet on the platform looking at the people inside pointing at him. Anyway, we got to the ground and he hung his big fur coat up on a peg but he didn't realise that the roof was leaking, because when he picked it up again, it was absolutely saturated. I must admit that at the time Watford seemed the place to be with Luther Blissett and co.- that's why I decided to go there on loan. I only played once for the first team as I got injured in training, so I left.

As soon as I'd gone, Bill Dodgin got back on the phone to me and said 'I told you to come to Brentford', so he persuaded me to come to Griffin Park. Dan Tana was the Chairman at the time too and was a bit of a character, I remember him telling me once that he'd seen Marilyn Monroe the night she died and was one of the last people to see her alive. But with regards to the football it was strange, in my first season after joining Brentford I got a promotion medal with Watford and Brentford because they both went up and I'd played for both sides.

I remember Brentford played Watford in the final away game of that promotion season and I was on the pitch before the game when Elton John came walking over and said 'I've got something here for you Doug' then produced my medal.

I'll always remember that game, we drew 1-1, but we should have got a penalty and won, which should have rounded the day off perfectly."

2002— Doug relaxed after a meal in Teddington

Dan Tana has received quite a lot of publicity in the national press about his relationship with the Hollywood stars. We haven't seen any of them down at Griffin Park though.

"There were quite a lot of showbiz faces about on match days back then because Willis Hall the playwright was a Director at the club. I remember he used to bring Michael Parkinson into the changing rooms before some games. I remember the Wednesday night after we got promoted we were supposed to be meeting the Mayor at the Hounslow Civic Centre and Bill Dodgin invited Willis Hall, Paul Shrubb and myself to go.

We all went to Willis Hall's club in London to have a meal and then planned to go on to the Civic function in Hounslow afterwards, but we all got drunk up at the club.

We started to come back towards Hounslow in a taxi, but Bill jumped out of the cab somewhere in the West End. The rest of us eventually made it back to the Mayor's do a bit worse for wear. We were walking around chatting, when all of a sudden, these big doors burst open and in staggered Bill Dodgin. It was brilliant!"

You were signed to complete Bill Dodgin's jigsaw - to give us more options down the left and give the forward line of Gordon Sweetzer, Steve Phillips and Andy McCulloch better service. What was the atmosphere like at Brentford when you joined?

"It was really good. When I joined it was leading up to the Christmas period and we did okay. I remember joining on the Wednesday, training on the Thursday and winning on the Saturday. It was a very friendly place to be."

With Jackie Graham out of the side Brentford had a dodgy January and slipped away from the promotion pace setters. But what was he like as a Skipper?

"Jackie was Brentford through and through. In training and on the pitch he never gave less than everything. He was really loyal to the club and probably should have made a move to see what he could have achieved. Jackie and myself both got released by Brentford on the same day.

1979— Fans show their appreciation towards the manager

I remember we were doing some training with Fred Callaghan and he didn't say a word, then I went home and a guy from the *Evening Standard* rang me up and said, 'I see you and Jackie Graham have been released?'

I told him he must have got his story wrong as we'd been training all morning with Fred and nobody had said anything to me. I think Jackie read that he'd been released in the newspaper, after all those years of service it was terrible. All the service the guy had given the club and there wasn't even a five-minute chat.

I think that is pretty typical of some football clubs though. When they want you they're all over you, but as soon as they don't want you any more, that's it. Dave Carlton went about the same time too. The reason Fred eventually gave us for letting us go was that he wanted to play a younger team.

It was a shame because we'd fought hard to avoid relegation. I played in all the games after Fred took over and we got out of trouble. As I say, it's like that at most clubs, I had the same at Millwall.

I was playing on a week-to-week contract as I wouldn't sign for Benny Fenton, then Gordon Jago came in for me at QPR and I thought I'd get a nice little move there. But a week later Benny Fenton got the sack and there was a chance to stay at Millwall again because Jago was given the Millwall job.

He told me that if I signed my contract and stayed at The Den he'd get the deal back-dated, so I signed and didn't get a penny. I should have twigged what was about to happen at Brentford because afterwards I remembered something the physio Eddie Lyons said to me.

I was on the treatment table having something done to my foot, and while he was working away on it he said to me, 'whoever treats your foot next should do this and that.'

I thought it was a strange thing to say at the time but didn't think any more of it. But they were happy days at Brentford."

When you joined Brentford you went straight into the side alongside Steve Phillips and Andy McCulloch who were both very good goal-scorers at that level weren't they?

"Yeah, with Andy you could put a ball into the box and he would go in for anything. He'd knock anything out of his way too which made things easier for me as I could just float a ball over and he'd get after it.

He was similar to a guy at Millwall called Alfie Wood - no matter where the ball was he'd go for it. Andy was brave and would just go steaming in.

Stevie Phillips was more of a poacher and would be after the knock-ins and picked off of Andy. But when I was at Brentford Stevie got the Adidas Golden Boot for being the top scorer in the country, which was amazing for a Fourth Division player."

Stevie Phillips always used to wear that yellow T-shirt under his Brentford top didn't he? What was all that about?

"[Laughs] Yeah, all the time. It was a superstition to him and something he always had to put on before a game, but it seemed to work for him. I'm not sure if he used to wash it actually!

He used to travel down from Northampton with Dave Carlton and Barry Tucker every day for training, they used to get away with a lot I remember."

Barry Tucker was the final addition to the promotion side and seemed to shore up the defence. Did he seem to make a big difference when he arrived?

"Yeah he was a solid little player, really reliable. Barry never used to do anything outstanding, but he was always there.

There was nothing of him really, but he was a lovely bloke."

So was there a buzz about the club when you joined. Did it seem like we were a team that was going up?

"Yes, we were always confident, especially at home I remember. I felt like we were always going to do well. The atmosphere in the dressing room was good, it was relaxed. Some players wouldn't come in until about a quarter to three, they would be outside talking then get changed late.

It was a great feeling to hear the buzz of the crowd as you were getting ready to walk out of the dressing room towards the tunnel, it really was. Bill would give a little team talk, but nothing too long.

He was a character Bill. I remember a couple of games when we'd been struggling and we'd come in at half time expecting to get a rocket from him, he said 'right, sit down', so we all sat down and he stood there with a note pad.

He then shouted, 'who wants to play golf and who wants to play squash on Monday?' And that was it! We thought we would get a right bollocking and all he asked was if anyone wanted to go to Fox Hills golf course.

But other times, when we'd been doing quite well, he used to slate us completely. Even the time I got sent off against Sheffield United he didn't say a lot, he called me in the next day and told me he'd tried to get me off of a longer suspension by telling the referee that I couldn't punch my way out of a wet paper bag."

So talk us through that bare-knuckle fist fight you had with Mickey Speight. It's been described as the best two-player brawl Griffin Park has ever seen.

"[Laughs] Well it wasn't funny really I suppose. It was a big match under the floodlights, I used to love games under the floodlights, and there was a very big crowd at Griffin Park that night. I kept getting the ball played out to me, I'd lay it off, then he'd come in late every time and whack me in the back.

That happened about half a dozen times I guess, so I turned round to him and warned him that the next time he did it I was going to kick him back. Anyway, it all happened again and it all went off just before half time.

We were rolling around all over the place and we ended up off the pitch. I was on the floor of their dug-out and their players and trainer were putting the boot in and stamping all over me.

Bill Dodgin and Tommy Baldwin jumped off of our bench and came into the Sheffield dugout to get me. All I could see were boots coming in - it was like a free-for-all at one stage.

So we eventually got out of the dugouts and back on the pitch and continued fighting over by the railings at the side.

I remember some of the fans in the Braemar Road stand were

holding this guy from behind against the fence, which I thought was quite handy. Anyway, the police came along and settled things down and told us to get away from the pitch and not to bother coming back out.

Bill didn't really say that much to me at half time, he didn't bollock me anyway. Afterwards, as I say, he said I couldn't punch my way out of a wet bag. I got home that night and I remember my dad, who couldn't make it to the game that night because he wasn't very well, had heard it mentioned on the news.

I remember him saying to me sarcastically, 'It sounded like you did really well with that sending off...' But that was only the second time I'd been red-carded."

Surely after 200 plus games for Millwall you must have been able to punch your way out of a wet bag?
"[Laughs] Yeah, you would have thought so. I used to get booked a lot at Millwall for my mouth, but not for kicking."

How different was Brentford to Millwall at the time?
"It was very different. Millwall was more professional I thought, it seemed a better organised club. Training was a lot stricter too, lots more fitness work and sprinting, but at the end of the day we had about the same amount of success.

All the players at Brentford loved Bill Dodgin and they wanted to do well for him. Benny Fenton, my old manager at Millwall, always used to slate the players, but that's something Bill would never do. At half time too, I can remember Benny having players up against the wall.

I played a game once where Eamonn Dunphy, a little scruffy bloke at the time who went on to become a multi-millionaire through U2, got involved in a really nasty incident.

At half time a big argument erupted in the Millwall dressing room and Eamon's picked up a bottle and smashed it on the side of the bath. But the wrong end of the bottle broke and he cut his hand!"

The Den was a horrible old ground wasn't it?

"Well, I don't know, as a home player it was great. We had a group of supporters who'd always used to 'greet' the away team coach before every match. I'm sure those guys used to give Millwall a two goal lead before we'd even started. People are always asking me at work what it was like knowing you had mad supporters who were behind you. I've got to admit, that it was a nice feeling.

I remember playing at Everton in the Quarter Finals of the FA Cup and we won 2-0. As the players got off of the train at Liverpool the noise was unbelievable. It was like a scene out of the film *Schindler's List*. All the way down the platform was a row of police and they were holding their snarling dogs back, it was really amazing.

The police were frisking a big group of Millwall fans up against a wall and next to them was a big pile of bats, knives and all sorts. I also remember playing in a game where Mark Lazarus, who had been at Brentford, was having a go at a Millwall legend Harry Cripps.

Anyway, all of a sudden, a lady jumped up over the barrier with an umbrella and she started laying into Lazarus with it. It was so funny... they were mad."

You describe Bill Dodgin as very laid back - as a player he must have been a dream?

"Well it was ideal for me because I was coming to the end of my career and it was lovely to go to a club like Brentford. Bill just let us get on with things. I used to live near the Robin Hood roundabout in Roehampton and Bill used to pick me up in his car before we caught the coach to some away matches.

I remember after we'd played down at Bournemouth and I'd been involved in a mix-up with one of the goals with Len Bond and we lost 3-2. It was pretty bad, I'd tried to play this ball back to Len and we collided leaving the ball in the middle of the goal and an empty net.

Anyway, on the way home in his car Bill told me from then on, what ever was happening on the pitch, I was never allowed back to defend...

'Just stay up field, you're more of a hindrance coming back' he told me. But Bill was a dream.

I remember once, we'd won a game on the Saturday and I got a phone call at home on the Monday morning from Bill. It had been pouring down with rain all weekend and Bill had this little stream running through the bottom of his garden in Byfleet.

He said to me, 'my stream is right the way to the top almost, I'll see everyone on Wednesday.' Or he'd say, 'I'll see you down the sauna at Isleworth.'

But from one week to the next you didn't know how to take him. He gave the job 100 per cent even though he did have a few relaxed methods. He used to keep me back in training sometimes and help me work on my crosses - we used to be there for about an hour and a half some days, banging balls into the area.

Bill Dodgin Senior, Bill's dad, used to turn up for training too sometimes. Training was only normally between 10.30 and midday though."

It sounds as if the team would have done better if he wasn't so relaxed about things. From a fan's point of view it doesn't sound like you really had to do much work during the week. I'm surprised any of the players were fit enough to last ninety minutes on a football pitch.

"[Laughs] Well, we did have to work, we used to train, but it was always with a ball. Some managers ran training like a boot camp and you'd dread training, especially during the pre-season month.

Bill used to take us over to Richmond Park before the season started and we did a lot of running, but Bill always used to lead the way and he'd tell us that nobody was allowed to overtake him."

What was Bill Dodgin's managerial partner, Tommy Baldwin, like in your opinion?

"Tommy and Bill seemed to have a nice understanding together. Everyone knew of Tommy because of his career at Chelsea and when I arrived he was still getting a few games for Brentford.

He was a quiet kind of bloke, nothing flash - he was a really nice fella. He used to take a lot of the training and get involved in a lot of the practice games.

I remember we used to go to Gunnersbury Park on a Friday which was about a ten minute walk from Griffin Park and train in what we used to call 'dog shit corner'.

It seemed as if we practised in the same corner that every Brentford dog owner took their animals. We used to dread it, not that I used to do many sliding tackles [laughs] but some of the defenders used to get in a right mess. Luckily for me I wasn't really a tackler."

What were away games like then, I assume you had to do a lot of over-nighters, as there were a fair few long journeys while you were a Bees player?

"If it was any real distance we used to travel up on the Friday and I used to share a room with Paul Shrubb.

At some clubs the manager would stop you drinking, but Bill would let us have whatever we wanted within reason.

He used to think that if we enjoyed a little drink at home during the week it was pointless stopping us having a pint the night before the game. Obviously nothing silly though."

At the end of your first season at Brentford we got promoted. Can you remember the scenes at the end of the 2-0 home win against Darlington that clinched it?

"I will always remember that day. The crowd went mad. I can remember leaving the ground at about 6 o'clock and we walked towards The Griffin Pub up the road on the left and it was really crazy, everyone was trying to get me to come in for a drink, it was brilliant.

After that the club said to us we could all go anywhere we wanted for a little holiday, but for some reason we all chose to go to Guernsey. We could have gone to Spain, Greece, anywhere really, but we ended up in Guernsey.

It was a good week away though with all the lads together and we played a game out there."

So you didn't all go out celebrating as a team when you clinched promotion?

"No, we all went our separate ways actually. It's funny, people think that footballers live in each other's pockets. We had a few drinks after the match in the bar, then went off home. In fact, I don't think we had a party to celebrate at all after going up."

Brentford are famous for going up and coming back down again, but we consolidated well in 1978 and it was an exciting season overall.

"I think a lot was down to the arrival of Jim McNichol, he made a big difference. I remember the fans singing 'Jiiiiimmmyyy' whenever we used to get a free kick around the penalty area and Jim used to walk up and take it.

He had a decent shot. Not a lot used to get past Jim McNichol and Pat Kruse, neither of them were that tall for central defenders but they were solid.

With Len Bond behind them, I don't think there were many better at that level. I remember Len Bond brought Ian Botham into the dressing room once, I think they went to school together."

It nearly went pear shaped in our second season back in the Third Division. Brentford were flirting a bit too closely with relegation, Bill Dodgin was given paid leave of absence and Tommy Baldwin was sacked.

Fred Callaghan came in and took the credit for keeping The Bees up, but do you feel that Bill would have turned things round if he'd stayed?

"Well, I don't know. I think it was a good time for someone to come in because the way we were going something had to change. All Fred really changed was working on the players' stamina. We did a lot more running in training and the sessions were really knackering.

But I think Bill was just unlucky - it wasn't the fact that we were doing anything that different under Fred, we were just going through a bad time. We had about half a dozen games left to avoid the drop and I think anyone could have taken over and things would have changed. That's what happens in football.

So it worked in Fred's favour really. Fred was alright, but he was nothing like Bill, nothing whatsoever."

So Fred Callaghan was a lot stricter with their players?

"Yes he was. We had to be at the training ground dead on time, whereas with Bill, if you were a bit late he'd understand. Bill didn't have a whip and he didn't crack down, but you did know where you stood with him. Bill had a lovely way about him and a lot of the time you'd want to play well for Bill if you know what I mean."

What sort of money were you on at Brentford?

"I think I signed on for about £200 per week, which wasn't bad back then, but we'd get a crowd bonus on top of that. I think we got something like £10 per thousand over 10,000 people. So if we did well and played the bigger teams we got a bit extra.

I've still got my first pay slip from Millwall too, £4 a week. I was an apprentice still and was cleaning boots every day of the week, but on a Saturday I was playing in the first team.

I remember, Keith Weller, who was in the side at the time, went to Benny Fenton the manager and said it was crazy to have me still scrubbing boots and baths when I was in the first team every weekend. I went up to £20 a week after that."

Do you still look out for Brentford's results?

"Along with Millwall's, I always keep an eye out and like to see Brentford do well. The only team that I've been at that I don't keep tabs on is Leyton Orient. I was with them for four years, but I knew straight away it was a bad move. I wasn't happy there.

If I got injured at Millwall or Brentford I'd try to get back as quickly as I could, but at Orient I'd let things drag on a bit. My heart wasn't really in it at all.

As I say, I do keep tabs on Brentford, but I don't really get the chance to get along to any matches because I get so few Saturdays off as I'm working shifts at Heathrow."

Dean Holdsworth

Date: Monday April 29th, 2002
Venue: The Reebok Stadium, Bolton
Era: 1989-1992 Appearances: 106 Goals: 49

One look at Dean Holdsworth's watch tells you all you need to know about his career since leaving Griffin Park. I'll leave your imagination to picture the car-priced timepiece, but we're not talking 'Swatch' here, I can assure you. Football has clearly made Deano a very, very rich man. His better days may be behind him now, and I'm sure the hunger isn't quite what it was, but Holdsworth is a household name and he commands superstar status at The Reebok Stadium.

Like most Brentford fans, I've always kept one eye on Dean's progress over the years. He's grabbed both the back and front page headlines in the tabloids since leaving, but I still consider Holdsworth to be one of us.

Okay, his time at Brentford may have just been a stepping stone, one which enabled him to move on to bigger and better things, but to most Brentford supporters he is the most influential player of the past decade.

We've had other prolific goal scorers, we've had other players who have gone on to grace the top level, even World Cups, but Deano actually delivered while he was at Griffin Park: Holdsworth took us where we deserved to be.

I'm positive that if Dean had been given the chance, or perhaps had the desire, to stay with The Bees for another season, he would have continued to score goals at a phenomenal rate and Brentford would have avoided being one-season-wonders in the First Division.

Perhaps delaying his departure would also have given him the chance to move to a Tottenham or an Arsenal, and a better chance of a full England call-up.

At Wimbledon, Deano certainly made his name, but the stigma The Dons carried throughout their Premiership years arguably restricted his chances of top honours. Not that Holdsworth probably loses too much sleep over the issue - he has still become a fairly big fish in a pretty big pond despite the influx of big name, foreign stars with whom he now shares his dressing room. Players like Youri Djorkaeff.

I caught up with Dean after Bolton's final home game of the 2001-2002 season, in the players' lounge following Arsenal's critical Premier League victory. With his trademark Armani baseball cap perched meticulously on his head, he welcomed the chance to reminisce about his time at Griffin Park. Holdsworth loves his role as folklore hero. But the Reebok Stadium, April 2002, was a million miles away from the last time I met him, husky racing on Hampstead Heath back in 1992.

When I interviewed you ten years ago, you made a pretty bold statement. We still had eight games to go and you claimed that if we avoided defeat against Bournemouth the next day, you thought we wouldn't get beaten for the rest of the season and would get promoted. Was that borne out of genuine belief in the camp that we were on the verge of something great?

"Yeah, there was an amazing atmosphere in the squad at the time, we had some really tough games ahead of us, but the feeling was that we could definitely go straight up. Looking back there were some really strong teams up there with us, and a few results went our way, but we knew we had the beating of any team in that division on our day and I felt that we were going to finish really strongly, which we did."

What a superb season the Championship season was for you personally, it established you as one of the country's brightest striking prospects didn't it?

"Yes it was a great season for me, especially after the injury troubles I suffered the season before. I had a torn thigh muscle and it was really causing me all kinds of troubles and restricted what I could do, how often I could play and how many goals I could score. When I joined Brentford I set myself the mission of scoring as many goals as I could to see where they took me, so to miss a lot of my first full season was a blow. I trained through

the whole of the close season and was feeling really fit and the new season started off very well. Me and Gary Blissett really gelled and with Neil Smillie and Marcus [Gayle] there too, we were a good attacking team, great on the break, with plenty of options."

It probably doesn't mean that much to you now after playing for so long in the Premier League, but was it a disappointment not to have beaten the club's goal scoring record that season?

"It means an awful lot to me to have equalled the post-war scoring record at Brentford. I was gutted to come off at Peterborough with a dead leg, as I was desperate to score. But to have equalled it was an achievement in itself."

The Brentford v Fulham match, for a lot of fans, was the game of the generation. With so much at stake and the game being such a hot local derby, what was it like to play in?

"Absolutely amazing. I can honestly say that the 4-0 win against Fulham was probably the most complete team performance I've been involved with. From start to finish we were in total control, and in the first half in particular, we would have beaten most teams in the country. Griffin Park was packed, the atmosphere was superb and we wiped the floor with Fulham. They had a chance of reaching the play-offs too and their players would have been really up for it, but we didn't let them have a sniff and scored all four goals in the first half. Fantastic!"

Your partnership with Gary Blissett played the pivotal part in our success, and he joined you at Wimbledon a year later. Did you get on well with Bliss off of the pitch too?

"Well we didn't really socialise off of the pitch much as he lived on the other side of London to me, but we definitely gelled on the football pitch. At Wimbledon Gary didn't really make the transition up a level and didn't get that long a run in the team along-side me, but he was a very good player as his scoring record shows."

Phil Holder had a few critics nearer the end of his reign at Griffin Park, but what was he like as a man motivator?

"Phil was a different class. He was great at man management and I really got on well with him. I keep in touch with Phil from time to time and the last I heard he was over with Steve Perryman again in Japan. I'm not sure if he's still over there, but all the players loved Phil and he definitely got the best out of us with the way he was."

Peterborough away is the stuff that dreams are made of for Brentford fans - nobody will ever forget the way events unfolded that day. What are your personal memories of that fantastic day?

"I really remember pulling up in the big car park outside the ground and seeing the place packed out with Brentford fans. There was Brentford everywhere and we all knew on the coach that this could be a special day. The fans were outstanding, the noise was superb and it lifted us to see so many fans waiting for us to come off the coach. On a personal level, as I said, I was really gutted not to have been able to score, but I'll always remember those scenes and the people on the pitch back at Griffin Park when we all got back to the ground."

Considering how much football has changed in the past decade, in particular the way Premiership clubs have stopped buying promising lower division players, do you feel you would have been given the chance to move up the leagues quite so quickly if you'd been starting off in the game now?

"It's hard to say really. Goal scorers still seem to get snapped up, but I may have been at Brentford longer, yeah. The thing was, though, that there wasn't much talk of me ever staying. It wasn't necessarily from me, I was happy to consider all my options as my contract was up and my club had got promoted.

In truth, I wasn't even offered a new contract by the club and felt they wanted me to go so they could get some money for me. I remember when we were on the open topped double decker outside the civic hall and fans were shouting up at me 'Deano, don't

Holdsworth & Blissett celebrate Brentford's promotion in 1992

March 1992— Holdsworth goes husky racing on Hampstead Heath

"I wasn't even offered a new contract by the club and felt they wanted me to go so they could get some money for me."

April 2002– Holdsworth wearing his trademark baseball cap

go, stay with us, stay with Brentford...' All I could do was just wave back. But I was thinking to myself, 'it's not really going to happen lads, I haven't even been offered a contract!'

I'd be lying if I said I would definitely have stayed, even if I had been offered a new deal, but when you aren't given the choice, then there isn't really a lot to think about is there? My personal opinion is that the Chairman wanted to sell me, whether the club needed the money I don't know, but that's how it was in my eyes."

Brentford beat Bolton on the Easter Bank Holiday en route to clinching the title... Looking around me at this amazing Reebok Stadium and witnessing Bolton playing on an even level with the new Premiership Champions Arsenal, it's upsetting for me to see how our two clubs are poles apart.

"Bolton has been transformed in the past ten years, it's a fantastic club to be at and I've really enjoyed my time here. If Brentford could have stayed up in Division One maybe things would be different but just looking around you it's obvious that Wanderers are a very healthy club now. It's funny how things worked out as I scored a lot of goals against Bolton before they signed me, I thought they considered I had it in for them."

There's been talk recently hinting you may move to Luton Town and join up with Joe Kinnear again. I'm sure it would be great to link up with your old manager, but hypothetically, what would it take for you to come back to Brentford? Would you consider dropping down the divisions again?

"I've got a year left on my contract at Bolton so it's just talk at the moment, but Joe has been in contact with me to talk about things. If I was to move anywhere it would only be to a club with real ambition, with a set-up that was moving in the right direction. I must admit, it would be good to be in a situation where I got a game every week and could be in a position to score goals as often as I'd like again, so we'll see. But I would only ever move down the divisons again if I felt the club I was moving to matched the ambitions I expect."

1965— Tommy scores during Brentford's 5-2 win over QPR

Tommy Higginson

Date: Friday 24th May, 2002
Venue: Tommy's House, Isleworth
Era: 1959-1970 Appearances: 435 Goals: 16

Life began for Tom Higginson in the little Scottish mining village of Newtongrange, eight miles from Edinburgh. His father was a miner and an aspiring footballer himself. On leaving school Tommy became a butcher and played for Edina Hearts in his spare time.

One Sunday his younger brother came running to tell him that Kilmarnock's manager, Malcolm MacDonald, a Brentford star himself after the Second World War, had called to see him and offered Higgy a trial the following week.

Tommy impressed and was snapped up straight afterwards. Before he'd kicked a ball for The Killies, national service called and Tommy saw active duty with the Royal Scots Regiment in Egypt during the Suez campaign.

Malcolm MacDonald had left Kilmarnock to take over the helm at Griffin Park before Tommy came out of the army two years later, but it obviously wasn't a case of 'out of sight out of mind' for his former manager.

In the summer of 1959 Higgy had another visit from MacDonald and was brought down to London. Higginson went on to become an intrinsic part of the Brentford squad for almost ten solid seasons. Those were halcyon days for Brentford. George Francis and Jim Towers were scoring at a phenomenal rate and the Brentford team almost picked itself. But Higginson's work rate and application in the reserves saw him break into the Bees first team and he never looked back.

At one stage Tommy clocked up 139 consecutive matches. Over four hundred games later, Higginson hung up his Brentford boots but he has never moved away from the area, working at Firestone's factory along the Great West Road and playing for Hillingdon Borough.

Tommy is a fiercely loyal and proud man - a true Brentford great. Not that Tommy sees himself in that mould - his ingrained modesty would never allow him to see his achievements that way. But in his softly spoken, broader-than-broad Scottish accent, his recollections show how deeply he cared for the club and how much he enjoyed his career at Brentford.

Tommy is currently recovering from a knee replacement operation and has now got a scar from thigh to shin as a permanent reminder of his efforts in a red and white shirt.

After Malcolm MacDonald joined Brentford from Kilmarnock as manager, he returned to Rugby Park to snap you up.

"Yes that's right, he signed me for Kilmarnock when I was eighteen just before I went into the army to do my national service. I did my two years in the army then went back to the football club when I was twenty.

He left for Brentford the year I came out, about three months into the 1957-58 season when he came down to Griffin Park. I was only part time with Kilmarnock, but I didn't play a lot of games that first season out as I had torn ligaments and I was off for about six months with that.

The second season wasn't a lot better and I only got about fifteen games in the reserves, so I decided I'd have to move if I wanted to stay in the game. After missing two seasons of my career in the services and with my injuries, I had missed almost four years of playing.

Willie Waddell was manager of Kilmarnock at the time, so I had a word with him and asked if I could leave and he said I could. I remember going to watch the first team one Saturday and the doorman came over to me in the stand and said that Malcolm MacDonald had travelled up to talk to me, so I turned round and there he was sitting at the back of the stand.

I went over to say hello to him and he told me he'd heard I was looking to move away and would I be interested in coming to Brentford.

I remember my face lit up and I said, 'yes, I'll come to Brentford' there and then, although I had no idea where Brentford was. And that was that! So I decided to come down to get fit, go full time and really give it a go as a professional."

2002— Higginson's leg following his knee replacement

So what did you think about Brentford and London after Kilmarnock back then?

"I was delighted and I used to get about as much as I could. I used to go to all the dog tracks around and watch the racing."

Where did you stay when you first came down to London?

"I was in digs for a while. The first place was near Boston Manor then I moved in with a family at the back of Northfields station. But I remember I wasn't getting fed as I wanted and I had to go to local cafes for a meal after training.

They were nice people and the house was clean, but I didn't like having to eat chips and stuff after training, so MacDonald sorted me out another place, living with pensioners. I needed to be well fed, which I was. I was a good eater in those days. Our pre-match meal back then was always steak."

You took a while to break into the first team though?

"Yes I took a wee while, I got a few games that first season, but in those days I was an inside-forward or half-back, which were similar positions, but it's all different now. Anyway, Jim Towers got injured and I played up front for a couple of games."

When you came onto the pitch covering for Jim Towers for the first time, the entire Brook Road booed you. It must have been a baptism of fire?

"Aye they did. Well, he was so popular. But you've just got to get on with it haven't you? Jim Towers was a big personality - he was a very good player. But I didn't get much abuse really, not that I remember.

Maybe I did [laughs] but a lot of the songs from the crowd sounded like just one big noise from the pitch, but I was a trier and I think the crowd liked me. Maybe I'm being big headed but I think I was alright."

After slipping back into your more accustomed positions you made either the number four or six shirt your own for virtually the next decade didn't you?

"The testimonial organisers had done a great job. Eric White and the team did me proud."

"Yes I suppose I did, although I remember being dropped once or twice and missed a few games. Whenever that happened I looked at it as a challenge to work harder and get myself back into the first team and stay there."

Brentford got relegated in your second season at the club; it must have been a big blow?

"Aye it was, but we came straight back up. I played over thirty games in the team that went down and stayed in the side that won the Fourth Division Championship in 1963. I played in every single game that season."

There was quite a lot of money spent on the team that won the title that season wasn't there?

"Yes that's right, we bought Billy McAdams, Johnny Brooks then a bit later on John Dick from West Ham and Jimmy Bloom-field the following season. It was good to be playing in the same team as them although I took nothing for granted.

There were always players trying to get into the team. There was good competition. But whenever I was out and trying to get back into the first team I always tried to give it everything.

I wasn't one for hiding. Some players don't want the ball if they're having a bad game, but I if I made a mistake, I made a mistake. I just got on with it."

The big name, big money signings must have been just what the club needed at the time? Jack Dunnett appeared to be happy to buy the club's way out of the basement?

"Oh aye, but I certainly didn't get much for signing, I think I got something like a couple of hundred pounds, something like that. But Dunnett the Chairman was an MP and he seemed happy to spend a lot of money, which was good for us.

The new players increased the competition for places among the home-grown players because the big names were automatic first team choices. Malcolm MacDonald wasn't going to drop any of those and he played them straight away after they joined the club."

So was there any resentment in the squad that these guys had come in and walked straight into the first team?

"No, not as far as I was aware. I suppose I was lucky as I'd just played about a hundred games on the trot so I was established. I think at one stage I played over 140 consecutive matches. I remember the run came to an end about ten games into the next season when I got 'rested', but then I went straight back into the team the next match.

I didn't have a problem with MacDonald for doing that. I liked him and he must have liked me. He signed me as a young boy, then hadn't seen me play much before coming back and buying me for Brentford."

What was Malcolm MacDonald like as a man?

"He was a fair bloke, you knew where you stood with him I think. If you played well you got in the team, but he was trying out various players at the time he dropped me. He was having a look at a young Scottish player called Willie Smith, but he never really made the grade and was released."

The year you won the Championship [1962-63] the season was frozen off for three months as Britain endured one of the coldest winters on record. How did that affect the team?

"Yes we were rushing to get the games finished at the end of the season. We still trained hard, using gyms and halls and we used to go over to Gunnersbury Park and train over there. The park was really snowy, but it was okay to run about.

The club used to put shingle round the outside of the pitch at Griffin Park too and we used to do a lot of running around there. But it was up to the individual. I've always enjoyed staying fit and it was up to the person if they wanted to stay fit."

After the football season resumed and the snow thawed Brentford got back to battling it out with Oldham at the top of the league and had nine games during April. One was against The Latics at Boundary Park where we lost 2-1 in front of 17,000 fans.

1960— Tommy establishes himself in the team

Match reports from the time say that Billy McAdams had a goal ruled out at the final whistle?

"I remember that well, that was terrible. Billy had scored and it would have been a draw so it was one point lost. The players weren't happy. We thought we'd got a draw, but there's nothing we could do about it. The ball crossed the line as the referee put the whistle in his mouth and blew full time. How could we change his mind and say if he was right or wrong though? Usually in the last minute the referee waits for the ball to go out of play or if there's a last minute corner they let the team take it, then, if it's cleared, they blow the whistle.

But we put the ball in the net from the corner and he blew too early. That decision could have meant the difference from winning the title or not winning the title and even who went up."

Luckily the 'goal' didn't matter too much and Brentford marched on to the Fourth Division Championship, we finishing the season with a cracking 4-3 win over Workington.

"Yes and I remember we were chasing the hundred goals in a season landmark. I think we finished one or two short. All the crowd were cheering us on to get the goals we needed. I think we needed six in the last game and missed the total."

What were the celebrations like after that game knowing Brentford had bounced straight back as Champions?

"Oh they were great. Everybody jumped onto the pitch. Going down and coming back the next season was just what we needed. The players all went out, some of them had a right good drink, but I just got washed and got home.

I've never been a drinker, some of them would get pissed though and I can't blame them! But it was good that we'd got back up in the one year."

There was a feeling that Brentford had bought their way out of that division.

"The Chairman Jack Dunnett had put a lot of money into getting us up and it paid off, but I don't know whether he was after the publicity or not. He was a crafty man and I remember he almost sank the club a few years later."

The crowds were great back then. Sixteen, seventeen and eighteen thousand fans almost every match, it must have been good playing in front of a packed Griffin Park?

"Yes the crowds were really good, but then again we were playing good football. They were a good team then, Brentford. That Championship team was certainly the best one I played in at the club and we played some good football. We carried on playing well too and in 1965 we almost went up again. It was touch and go for a while and we almost made it up to the Second Division. We did the double over the Champions Carlisle too - we scored six against them at Griffin Park."

Malcolm MacDonald decided to move back up to Scotland and Tommy Cavanagh took over. It must have been strange to see MacDonald go after following him to The Bees?

"Obviously he'd made his decision and he certainly wasn't thinking of me when he moved back to Scotland. He'd had a fair few years in charge of the club and he'd been a Brentford player in the 1930s and I think he wanted to go back to Kilmarnock.

He wanted to wait until the end of the season before leaving I think but the club let him go early and he went a couple of months early. We would have gone up that season but we had really bad results over Christmas, Brentford always seem to get a bad spell over that period."

Things took a turn for the worse at cash-strapped Brentford in 1967. What was the atmosphere like at the club from a player's point of view when QPR made their bid for the club?

"Well, we couldn't really do anything ourselves. There were fund-raising things and all that, but we wanted to play good football to get better crowds in.

We wanted to be successful for the supporters and get the attendances up. Obviously the better the crowds were the better it was for the club."

You personally got heavily involved in the fund-raising events didn't you?

"Yes, I walked from Brighton to Brentford and did alright. I was walking with some of the boys for a lot of the way, but it wasn't all of the players, just a certain few. We went down on buses to Brighton and I got in with a crowd of people near the front but eventually they became really tired and started stopping and that. I thought to myself, 'it's nay good this yer nar, I'm alreet...' So I kept on walking.

Eventually I caught up with a young boy, but then he dropped out so I pushed on myself. I didn't realise that I was at the front, but I was running for a little bit, then dropped to a walk, then ran for a bit and so on. My legs were getting a bit too tight just walking, so it felt easier running at times.

Then I got a bit mixed up with the roads, missed a turning somewhere and got off the line, that could have been a disaster. I eventually found myself around Twickenham and I remembered how to get back from there, but I was happy not to have got really lost after walking non-stop for twelve hours. I didn't set out to win the walk, but I just wanted to get it over and done with in the end.

I'm glad I won the race to tell you the truth, that way I've always remembered it. I was alright with blisters too because I had big heavy boots on."

Can you remember what kind of money you were on back then, were Brentford good payers?

"Oh, not a great deal really. But I was never really one for pushing for more money I was happy to be in a good job. I think later I was on about £30 per week, which wasn't bad, but Johnny Haynes was the top earner in England following the removal of the maximum wage and was the first £100 per week man.

When I came down from Scotland I think I was on about £18. But money never bothered me, I've never been a greedy bloke, wanting this and that. I took what they gave me."

We're back in a similar position to the crisis in 1967 again

right now, but do you keep up to date with events at Griffin Park as you're still living just up the road?

"Yes I keep up to date through the local 'papers and that but not in too much detail. I did think about going to Cardiff for the Play-Off Final, but I can't drive because my leg is still hurting a bit after my knee operation. I couldn't face sitting down on a train or a coach."

You were incredibly consistent at Brentford, clocking up around 450 appearances in just ten seasons. What was your secret to staying injury free for the best part of a decade? Yours was an incredible record.

"That's true and more often than not in the game where I didn't play during that time I was fit enough to have turned out if I'd been selected. I had torn ligaments while I was at Kilmarnock, but then you just played on. There were no substitutions back then so you had to soldier on even though you should have come off - I could have saved myself months of rehabilitation."

Do you think that perhaps your national service stint helped with your fitness later on in your career? Nowadays they say youngsters play too much football but your enforced absence from the game maybe helped you in the long run?

"Well, I'm not sure about that. It's true that I didn't really start playing that much until I was 22, but it's true I was still playing Sunday football well into my fifties. I've never smoked or drunk really, maybe a shandy now and again, but I've only been drunk about four times in my whole life and that was in the army.

Neither has really appealed to me. I've always been a runner, as a boy I never walked, I always ran. I did a lot of cross-country running in the army and I won medals for it.

Up in Scotland I did professional running too, in the Border Games. I used to take part in all the half-mile, mile and sprint races every week. I remember winning £65 in a handicap race up there, which was a lot of money when I was eighteen in 1955.

I ran the half-mile race in one minute, fifty-one seconds and I've still got the medal on the wall in my hall."

The fans certainly repaid your loyalty at your testimonial game, 6,500 people paid to get in to Griffin Park to see the game against QPR. You must have been very pleased with the turn-out?

"I was very lucky, yes. Especially as the crowds that season hadn't been very good. I thought there were more than 6,500 people at the game though, but I was glad with what I got. The testimonial organisers had done a great job. Eric White and the team did me proud.

They didn't just arrange the game with QPR, there were quizzes, dances and fund-raising all that season."

Were you worried about the future after your testimonial was over and you'd retired from the professional game?

"Well, I was a trained butcher so I thought I could go back to that. When I left school I had a milk round for about six months, then my father told me about a butcher's job he'd heard about just down the road, so I went for that and worked there for a couple of years.

So I went back into butchery eventually after Brentford, but not straight away, I got a job at Firestone for about three years. I left there in 1973. I was still playing football at the time.

I was coming off of the night shift at two o'clock in the afternoon then playing football for Hillingdon Borough. Other times I'd be rushing back from Hillingdon away matches so I'd be at work at ten o'clock at night. This went on for about three years. I enjoyed it obviously, earning extra money, but it was a killer.

Christ almighty, playing football and doing shift work too. But I was better off at Hillingdon than I was at Brentford, moneywise. Hillingdon were paying me £15 or £16 per week and that was on top of my Firestone money, but I would have loved to have stayed on at Brentford full time. I was proud of Brentford and always gave 100%.

We had some good cup runs at Hillingdon and got to the FA Vase Final at Wembley and played in front of about 30,000. The top Southern League sides then were Wigan Athletic and Hereford, but I remember beating both of them with Hillingdon.

2002— Tommy plays with his pet spaniel at home

Eventually I played for Syon Villa on Sundays, then I started running the team my boy played for, just training them and trying to help them. Then after he packed in I went back to Sunday football with another local side and we won a few bits and bobs in the Chiswick and West Middlesex leagues.

I think I was fifty-three when I stopped, but eventually I thought 'Christ, what am I doing running about here at my age?' So I packed it all in. I had my time in the game, I wouldn't change any of it, I've enjoyed my life."

So have you always been a football player rather than a football watcher? Do you watch football on TV at all or go along and watch games?

"No not really, that has never appealed to me. I've only been to watch a handful of games that haven't involved the teams I have been playing with. I was at the game where England beat Scotland 9-3 years ago, but I've always been daft on playing football.

I sometimes watch it on the telly, but if it isn't a good game I'll just turn it off. To be honest there's so much football on these days you don't know what to watch. A lot of the time, I prefer to go into the other room and read a book. Some people watch it all day every day and never get off their backsides do they?"

You played for the same club for eleven years, which is a high level of commitment to any club. Players nowadays are always on the move. What do you think about that?

"They're always on the move because that's how they make money, that's what it is. But now, with all the clubs on the verge of going under, it may stop.

I read in the newspapers a couple of times that other clubs were interested in signing me while I was at Brentford, but the club never came to me and told me that they wanted me to leave as another team had made an offer.

There were a few tit bits in the 'papers, but you never knew if they were true or not."

2001– Ingimarsson wins a header during Brentford's clash with QPR

Ivar Ingimarsson

Date: Thursday 9th May, 2002
Venue: Brentford Training Ground, Tolworth
Era: 1999-2002 Appearances: 135 Goals: 11

Ivar Ingimarsson, like many Icelandic players, exudes intelligence and motivation. Hard working, unpretentious, studious and modest, Ivar fully deserves every bit of success his fledgling career has brought him so far - in two words: model pro.

Ivar was signed by Ron Noades in October 1999 for £150,000 from IBV Vestmannaeyjar in Iceland, but struggled to establish himself in midfield. Steve Coppell's arrival brought the best out of the 25-year-old though - coupled with a switch back to the centre of defence - and Ingimarsson became the team's most consistent player and epitomised the spirit in the squad.

Unfortunately the time-honoured tradition of Brentford's Player of the Season leaving the club weeks after picking up the trophy was continued during summer 2002 and this interview with Ingimarsson was the last conducted as a Brentford player.

It was only a matter of time before the bigger clubs pounced, with Ingimarsson's superb form throughout the season attracting attention - especially as his regular inclusion in the Icelandic national team had raised his profile even further.

With the Euro 2004 qualification group matches about to start, it was important for Ingimarsson to be playing at the highest level possible to cement his place in the national team - and at the end of the day Brentford's defeat at The Millennium Stadium meant the player had to move on. Wolverhampton Wanderers eventually tempted him away from Griffin Park on a Bosman.

We caught up with the Supporters and Players' Player of the Year at Brentford's training ground in Tolworth just three days before the club's traumatic Play-Off Final with Stoke in Cardiff.

Spirits were still high on the training pitch when I visited and I feel the interview gives a unique insight into life in the Bees camp just days before their season came crashing down, the promising team was decimated and Steve Coppell walked out on the club.

Firstly congratulations on a superb season, 2001-2002 was a great success for you. What do you put that down to?

"I agree, it's been a very good season for me and obviously the team. It's been an amazing season compared to the last one.

We finished eighteenth last year but this time we have been competing in the top six throughout. We owe a lot to The Gaffer [Steve Coppell] who has made a massive difference."

Having Steve Coppell's experience at the club has obviously helped you personally?

"Yeah, definitely. It's helped playing in the same position for the whole season, especially when you are preparing for a game as you know exactly what your job is.

Obviously I've been put in the defence now and it has worked out very well."

You clearly seem to prefer life in the back four instead of being in midfield?

"Yes I do, but I think it's been a little bit down to the fact that I was also playing on the right or left of the midfield too.

I always thought I was a more central player, either in midfield or defence. I enjoy it more and I think that has shown this season and has worked well."

It looks at this stage that you are on the verge of becoming an established part of your national side. You must be excited at the thought of competing in the qualifying games for the Euro 2004 tournament?

"Yes, it's been great. Obviously it has a lot to do with the success that Brentford have had. It brings the spotlight on to the individuals in the team and it is a great honour for me to be called up.

It has always been my ambition to play for my country and it looks as though I've been able to force myself into it.

It's good to play in high profile internationals when everybody is available for selection. It's very good to be included in squads from my point of view."

You like to score goals in the first game of every season, you've done it for the past two years [Northampton 2000-01, Wigan 2001-02], is there any chance you can manage one in the last- this Saturday against Stoke at Cardiff?

"[Laughs] That's true, yes. I would be really happy if that would happen, but we'll just have to wait and see! I will definitely give it a go. It's hopefully my turn to score, there's a big connection with Stoke with their Icelandic owners and players and the game is on live TV in Iceland, so it would be nice to put one in the net. It would be the icing on the cake to score a goal there and wave home."

Will there be much conversation with the other Icelandic players on the pitch during the game, little insults and a few swear words exchanged as you run past each other?

"No, not really, you just concentrate on the game. Maybe you get the chance to chat before the match and say hello and that's it and you have to go out and try to win. There could be a few comments made in the temper of the game but afterwards it's fine we all get on very well, but when the teams are on the pitch both teams want to win."

We've already had two very tough games against Stoke this season, the one at Griffin Park in particular was very physical with lots of off the ball incidents going on. Will there be any 'history' taken into the match in Cardiff?

"Yeah, that's true the game at Griffin Park was a little bit different because they lost a player early on, but the away game was a really good match. It was a fast game with some good football being played and hopefully the final will be the same way. I hope it's a good game and hopefully in the end we'll get the right result."

This is the biggest game in every Brentford player's career isn't it?

"Yes, this game can change lives and it will make a lot of difference for Brentford as a club too. Everybody knows there is a

2002– Ivar accepts the fanzine's Player of the Season trophy

2001– Ivar during The Bees' F.A. Cup defeat at Scunthorpe

lot riding on it but you can't be thinking about things like that, you've just got to go for it and hope you do your best on the day and that it's enough to get the right result.

I haven't heard of any sleepless nights yet, but I'm sure someone has difficulty though. Myself, I'm just looking forward to it because it is a big, big occasion and I'm just going to enjoy every minute of the final."

So are you going to be eating any puffins before the big match? [puffins are an Icelandic culinary delicacy]

"[Laughs] I doubt it... As much as I want to, they'd be good for a pre-match meal!"

I interviewed Hermann Hreidarsson a couple of years ago and he told me he used to go out killing puffins on the Icelandic cliffs as it's almost a national sport over there. Are you a puffin murderer too?

"[Laughs] Yeah, yeah, I've done it many times! It's very of the culture actually - to catch a puffin and have a good meal."

It's not something you've tried since being over in England is it? You don't go out trying to catch pigeons or anything?

"[Laughs] No! I think you'd be locked up if you tried to do that here! Yeah we do that over there, it's just like eating a chicken I think, but a bit more colourful and a better taste!"

So how does it feel to have won every Brentford Player of the Season trophy?

"It was a huge honour for me, really. It proves to me that I must have been doing things right and for the fans to vote for me as their player of the season is something I am very proud of."

1989— Feeley at Ewood Park against Blackburn Rovers

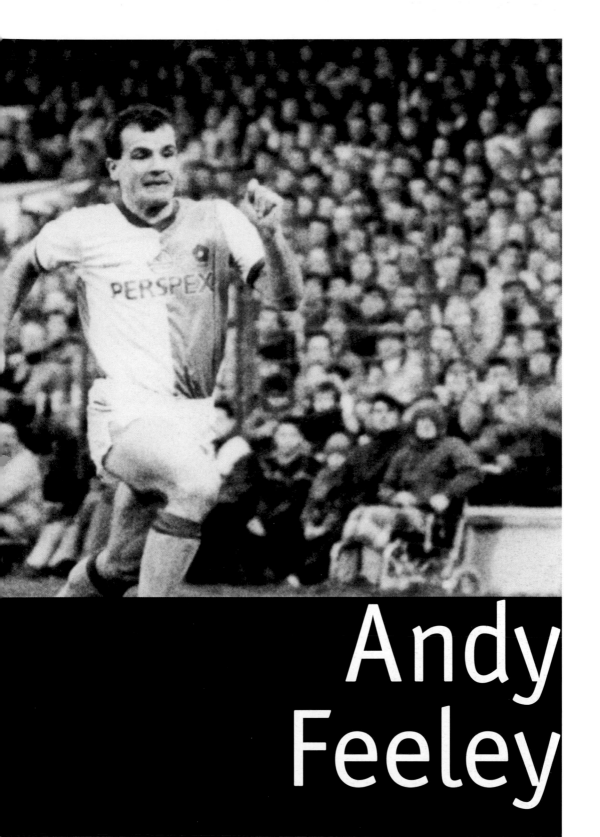

Andy
Feeley

Date: Tuesday April 30th, 2002
Venue: Gigg Lane, Bury
Era: 1987-1989 Appearances: 88 Goals: 0

Andy is serving the second football apprenticeship of his life and this one, I would imagine, is every bit as tough as his first at Leicester City back in the late seventies. Feeley has a hectic workload at Gigg Lane. As Director of Youth, the former Bees hard man is not only in charge of Bury's Centres of Excellence (looking after the eight to sixteen-year-olds) but is also Youth Coach (in charge of the sixteen to nineteen-year-olds)... Oh, and the reserve team too. I'm sure you'll agree that is some workload, but one that Feeley is relishing, even when he considers the horrendous season his club has endured. Relegation and administration became Bury's 'alternative double'.

Feeley may look like the tabloid portrayal of an England fan, with his St. George hat and arms adorned with tattoos, but this skinhead is dedicated to saving football at the grass roots, not picking fights. Listening to Feeley's passionate views on how football is being ruined by 'immoral' TV revenue distribution and the Premiership clubs' foreign player fetish, you feel that Andy definitely has a grasp of where football is failing and what needs to be done to rectify its demise.

It is so refreshing to meet an ex-player with so much passion and energy for the game. Football desperately needs more people like Feeley who can lead by example and shape the future of clubs like Bury, who, although suffering hard times, deserve their right to survive and ensure the national game remains in the heart of suburban communities and not just souless multi-million pound franchises.

You were part of the Brentford side that reached the last eight of the FA Cup in 1989. For a Second Division club to reach that stage and play at Anfield was amazing wasn't it?

"Yeah, we did really well to get there. We played Blackburn Rovers in the League Cup earlier in the season and we lost the tie in the away leg fairly heavily but then we took them to pieces back at our place, so we knew we had the beating of them when we drew them. We played really well at Ewood Park, and obviously we had the 3-1 win against Manchester City at home which gave us even more belief. So we were confident that we could win at Blackburn. Then we got Liverpool at Anfield and I honestly believe to this day that if we'd got drawn against any of the other teams left in the cup, we would have gone even further. Nottingham Forest and Everton would have been winnable I think, we were just the unlucky ones that got Liverpool."

What do you remember about the Liverpool game, the reception and the atmosphere at Anfield?

"It was unbelievable. Although we lost 4-0 our fans were superb and to be fair Liverpool were good to us. But I suppose you would expect that from Liverpool fans. They realised what an achievement it was for us to get there, and they gave us a great reception, clapping us off at the end. During the game I think tiredness set in and we conceded two late goals, to be honest the score flattered Liverpool I thought. But we performed well.

I knew that I'd never get the chance to play at Anfield again. I'd played there several times before with Leicester and had always done well, beating them a couple of times, so I knew what the atmosphere was like and what to expect. But when you think you will be going back again next year you don't take it all in. When you realise it's probably the last time you'll play there you try to absorb everything.

To be fair we could have taken the lead too. Richard Cadette went really close, we caused them all sorts of problems first half. I don't think we had a save to make. There were a few scrambles in and around our area but nothing clear-cut. Tiredness caught up with us in the end and their superior fitness showed. Obviously the touch of class of John Barnes and the like made the difference too. They were the best team in the country at the time."

In many respects Blackburn away will be remembered more than the Liverpool match. We played Rovers off of the park.

2002— Andy plays an important role at Gigg Lane

"I agree we were by far the better side on the day and we knew we were as good if not better than them, so we had no fear. We just went out and played and I think the score-line flattered them a lot. I think we could have run out very comfortable winners. We did take the piss to be fair.

It was the same against Manchester City at home. I never really thought we were in danger in that game either. It was in the first three rounds of the FA Cup run where I thought we were in more danger of losing.

Playing against Peterborough and Walsall was where we were more likely to go out rather than any of the later games, but I always felt comfortable. Most of the people round here support Manchester City, so I do get the chance to remind them of that match now and again."

The cup run ending as it did seemed to burst the Brentford bubble. We were still in with a shout of promotion and winning the Sherpa Vans, but we struggled from Anfield onwards. The sale of Andy Sinton couldn't have helped though?

"I think over the course of the whole season, we should have done better. We under achieved in a way. The Cup run was great, but we should have gone up because we were definitely one of the better sides in that division.

We should also have gone further in the Sherpa Vans, but we had that many games at the end of the season that it just disappeared. We lost some silly games, chucked silly points away and didn't really reflect the cup run in the league.

If we'd performed as we did against City and Blackburn more often, there were no sides who could live with us. Whether they be Wolves or Brighton, or any other side that was good at the time, we were equal to any of them.

As for Andy Sinton, you could never be surprised that he went because he was quality. The timing could have been better perhaps, but the club maybe needed the money, and since I've moved over to the coaching side of football at Bury, I can now appreciate the financial demands more than I did when I was a player.

Blackburn 1989— Andy Feeley and Terry Evans move in for the kill

"I honestly believe to this day that if we'd got drawn against any of the other teams left in the Cup, we would have gone even further."

You always think that a club should hold on to a player until the end of the season, but maybe there were circumstances that wouldn't allow that. Sinton couldn't turn down that move anyway, it was a bit sad that he went to QPR though. I thought he could have done a lot better. In the end he was signed by Tottenham Hotspur anyway.

You never know if we'd have gone up if Andy could have stayed, a player of his quality makes a lot of difference, but whether it would have been enough, who's to say? I would have liked to have thought so, but that's looking on the optimistic side of things. He was a good player and to be fair to him, the chance came and he took it. Andy was a great kid and the time was right for him to go personally, but obviously it left the rest of us a bit flat.

I think if we could have gone out and bought a couple of players with the money or got someone from QPR as part of the transfer then you could have accepted the deal. A fresh face would have bolstered the side, but perhaps Steve Perryman also thought we could go up without Andy? Knowing Steve he would have thought about it."

It wasn't all about Andy Sinton though was it? There were some other great individual players in that team. Who do you recall being the outstanding ones of that generation?

"Keith Millen. He was always a good player as his career since has showed. He did well at Watford and now at Bristol City. Keith Jones was excellent, but you're right, there were a few; Gary Blissett, Marcus Gayle, Dean Holdsworth and Richard Cadette.

There was none more talented than Richard Cadette at Brentford. There must have been something wrong with him somewhere, I don't know, but he should have done better with the ability he had.

On his day he was unstoppable, but he should have played at a higher level in England. I know he had a spell at Sheffield United and went up to Falkirk after Brentford, but he was the best I've seen for individual ability in a forward. Things didn't seem to work out as they should have for him though."

How did you rate the Perryman-Holder combination?

"They were different class. They are the best I ever played for, still to this day, Steve's knowledge of the game, the way he treats players, talks to players, from the kids upwards. He's a gent and I wish him well. I wish he would come back to English football now, I think we're missing someone like him.

I don't think he was given a fair crack at Tottenham. I spoke to him in the summer, I think he'd come back tomorrow if the right opportunity arose."

With you and Terry Evans in the side, that Brentford team didn't take many prisoners did it?

"[Grins] No we didn't, we could look after ourselves! I think there was a misunderstanding about Steve Perryman. Some people thought he was a bit soft, but he was ruthless. He could play, but he could sort people out too. That's what he wanted his teams to do. He wanted us to play, but when it was time to show the opposition the other side of the coin, he wanted us to do that as well.

When he was playing at Tottenham he had players around him like Dave Mackay so when there was a battle, they could win it.

I think you've got to do that in football even to this day. If you look at any of the top sides, they battle harder than anyone and that's what Steve wanted. I don't think he liked anyone taking the piss. Steve was still playing the odd game when I arrived. He came back as sweeper against Southend in the Cup if I remember, but I'd played against him while he was at Spurs and he was excellent. He was still the best player in training... By a mile. Nobody could get near him, his technique, his brain, he was superb and could do anything with the ball."

Memories of Anfield must seem a million miles away from the situation you've experienced at Bury this season?

"Yeah, without a doubt. You can't compare the two extremes. The top clubs are getting richer and the bottom clubs are left floundering. If something isn't sorted, whether they regionalise the lower divisions or reassess where the money goes, then I can see part time football. Definitely in the Third Division and

2002— Andy is kept very busy at Bury

maybe the Second. I'm not sure the people running the game are bothered, I think those in control feel that there are too many football clubs and they are very greedy. English football will definitely suffer, without a doubt.

I can see there only being forty full time football clubs, so where are the kids going to play? Even now there's no room for them all. Look at Arsenal's youth side with nine foreigners in it. That can't be right.

Up here our best youth players go straight into the first team, we've used a couple of seventeen and eighteen-year-olds this season and they know there's a path for them. My friends who work at Blackburn and Manchester United tell me that once they've finished at under-19 level, there's nowhere to go.

At Blackburn the reserves are all internationals, so there's probably twenty or so kids there who, like Ben Burgess, can't even get a game in the reserves, so they just do nothing. That's something that is happening at all the academies, it's so self-defeating. It's becoming a massive problem, they get pampered, they expect to get looked after.

From the age of sixteen all they do is play football, their dinners, their food, their clothes are all taken care of by the club. When they come out of that environment and come down to somewhere like Bury, where they have to take their kit home to wash it, buy their own boots maybe, they don't want to know.

Brentford were lucky with Ben Burgess, Rovers didn't want clubs up here to know about him because he'd be on their doorstep as a permanent reminder that the system is failing up here."

Listening to your job description it sounds as if the club should be reported. How do you fit everything in?

"It's a brilliant job and I'm lucky not to be at a bigger club as I wouldn't be able to get so involved. Some clubs have a vast team of people to look after a work-load like mine. I get to see the kids from eight years old until they're nineteen and some of the kids who joined when I started four years ago are now breaking into the first team and I've seen them progress all the way through. It's been a great experience."

1978— McCulloch celebrates in style with the Brentford fans

Andy McCulloch

Date: Monday 30th July, 2002
Venue: Marnie's, Weston Green, Surrey
Era: 1976-1979 Appearances: 122 Goals: 49

Ask any Brentford fan around the age of 32 or older, about the team when they first started to come to Griffin Park and they'll start waxing lyrical about Andy McCulloch.

Andy is another player who stands squarely in the Cult Hero category. A classic, big side-burned, seventies goal machine. Andy had all the ingredients to make him a massive hit with the Brentford faithful. Some of the headers he went in for were verging on suicidal.

The former QPR, Cardiff and Oxford striker was stretchered off more than once in a Brentford shirt for going in where it really hurt and with 'kamikaze' Gordon Sweetzer alongside him, our opponents' rearguard were always in for a torrid ninety minutes.

But for all his aerial power, height and strength, Andy was a natural finisher with the ball at his feet too and was an unselfish player in the area.

McCulloch forged a great partnership with the pint-sized Steve Phillips during the 1977-78 season, and although it appears there was little love lost between the pair away from football, the partnership bagged a phenomenal 58-goal haul during The Bees' march to promotion.

When you consider that Gordon Sweetzer also scored 14 goals during that campaign, you can imagine what an exciting era Bill Dodgin's style of flowing football brought to Brentford.

But to the despair of the fans, Andy was sold to Sheffield Wednesday for £60,000. I met Andy, his wife and daughter on a hot summer's evening in the garden of Marnie's Pub in Weston Green just off the A3 in Surrey.

Most fans remember your 'golden' partnership with Stevie Phillips under Bill Dodgin, but it was John Docherty who brought you to Griffin Park. How did you find life at Brentford in the early days?

"Well it was a great club to be at after Oxford, the social scene and the atmosphere between the players was superb. I'd never been anywhere before where people were so close.

Everyone used to go out after every home game, all the players and their wives. We'd either all go out to a restaurant or somebody would have a party at their house, it was fantastic.

I've been at seven league clubs, but Brentford was by far the most friendly. We went out every week, win or lose, there was just a great spirit there. John Docherty bought me on an 'injury clause' but I was delighted to leave Oxford United.

I had some terrible treatment there. Some 'Billy Whiz' doctor thought he was a miracle worker and wanted to get me back in three weeks after having my cartilage taken out. He was a new doctor on the scene who thought he could do anything, so after I had the cartilage removed, they put my leg in plaster and just sent me home.

Then it really blew up and I was rushed back to hospital. They ripped the plaster off and they had to aspirate the knee because it was haemorrhaging, so instead of being out for three weeks, I ended up being out three months and I could have lost my leg. I think I had terrible treatment there.

That's one of things I regret about not playing today, all the medical people in the game know how to treat injuries properly now. Players are rested if they're not fit. Half the time, because I was Oxford's record signing, I was made to play and normally I was only about 80% fit. John Docherty was a real motivator and coach though. He was a good manager."

Were you more confident with the medical treatment you received at Brentford?

"I was delighted to be treated by John Lyons and Dr. Radley-Smith at Brentford. They did another operation, which they got right to a certain extent. But the Chairman, Dan Tana, wasn't that happy with me coming to Brentford as he thought I was too much of an injury risk. Once I had got over the injury, got back to playing football and started scoring a few goals, it was great and I really enjoyed being at Brentford.

The physio Eddie Lyons was a lovely man, a real character. I heard he was related to one of the Bee Gees or something? Every morning, without fail, when we were arriving for training, he would come up to me and say, 'alright Andy, what did you have for breakfast?'

And before I'd had the chance to give him a reply, he'd say, 'well I had three sausages, four rashers of bacon, two eggs, four tomatoes, three rounds of toast....' Every single morning he said that, to everyone. He was lovely, he used to play the spoons and do his tap dancing too, Eddie was a real one-off."

So moving to Brentford allowed you to wipe the slate clean and start again really?

"I'd been lucky to have been at some good clubs before Oxford. I'd been at QPR, which was an interesting club, and then I enjoyed my time at Cardiff. But Cardiff decided they needed the money and had to sell me. Oxford paid them a record fee of £75,000 at the time.

It was funny, I joined Oxford at the time when Holland had the famous 'total football' style with Cruyff, where full backs and defenders were encouraged to attack and come forward.

The Oxford manager, Gerry Summers, wanted to try it too, but unfortunately [laughs] didn't quite have the players to do it. It just didn't work out there really. I scored one or two goals, but I didn't really enjoy it and was glad to get away.

It took me about six months after joining Brentford to really get going though, but I loved the fans at Griffin Park and I think they understood and appreciated somebody who gave 100%."

The fans were very fond of you at Brentford weren't they?

"The banter with the crowd at Brentford was different class. The rapport with the supporters is something I've never forgotten. I was told that a lot of the lads who used to stand in a certain part of the ground were market traders from the old Brentford market and they used to come to the games straight from their stalls or via the pub.

Some of the language was amazing [laughs]. One comment I

heard there stopped me dead in my tracks during a match. I'd missed a shot and was jogging back towards the middle when somebody shouted out 'that was awful McCulloch, you're as bad as your father was'.

[Laughs] I was so shocked that anyone remembered that my dad was a footballer too and that the guy had been able to insult the pair of us in the same sentence!

You'd never want to get on their bad side though. Stevie Phillips' wife used to stand up and have blazing arguments with the fans when they said something she didn't like. It was really funny. She used to shout at them 'don't you dare say that about my husband, he's playing really well today'. But I always told my wife never to argue with the supporters as they'd paid their money and were entitled to their opinions."

Have you heard from Steve Phillips since you left?

"No I haven't. No disrespect to him, but out of all of the players at Brentford, I was least friendly with Steve I'd say."

The season Brentford got promoted [1977-78] the McCulloch, Phillips, Sweetzer combination scored 72 goals. What games from that season stand out in your memory now?

"The Easter period still stands out to me I think. We won five games on the trot and the pressure was on. We knew we had to win the home games during that stage if were going to have any chance of going up and we did really well.

I scored a few during that run too [one against Newport County away and two versus Stockport at home] which was great. I remember Dan Tana coming up to me after we'd won promotion and telling me that he was wrong to think I wasn't a good signing for the club when I first arrived.

He said he'd been really impressed and we became really close friends after that. Our wives got on really well too which was an added advantage."

Dan Tana was certainly another character wasn't he. What was it like having such a colourful Chairman?

"Well he certainly looked after us, especially after we'd won promotion. I was lucky enough to be a guest of his over in America once or twice and he was a very friendly and generous man. He was extremely well connected in America and everyone seemed to know him.

I'll never forget going horse racing with him over there - let's just say that he didn't lose many races. Once he knew other clubs were starting to look at me and he thought I may be thinking of looking at my options, Dan helped me to set up a summer spell in America and tried to keep me as happy at Brentford as he could."

At the end of the promotion season, instead of taking a well-earned rest, you went over to America and played for the Oakland Stompers. What was that like?

"That was a very strange few months. Nobody in the whole squad seemed to gel at all. But I guess that was almost impossible really, when you only have three months to get to know each other and have players coming in from all over the place.

But I remember the clubs were really trying to attract families along to watch the games and there were some very unusual half-time events. One game they had all these performing elephants on the pitch during the break and in the second half we had to try and avoid all their muck that was left on the pitch.

In another game Michael Jackson came in to the dressing room and handed out all this merchandise stuff. It was embarrassing because none of the players took any of it - we all thought he was a right weirdo."

Which players at Brentford did you rate?

"Jackie Graham was a good captain. He wanted to win and was a real motivator. Jackie was a great Elvis impersonator too. But week in week out he was a player I knew I could rely on and I think Jackie was a very good player. Dave Carlton was another good player too.

He was one of Bill Dodgin's prodigies, Bill loved him because he could play a bit.

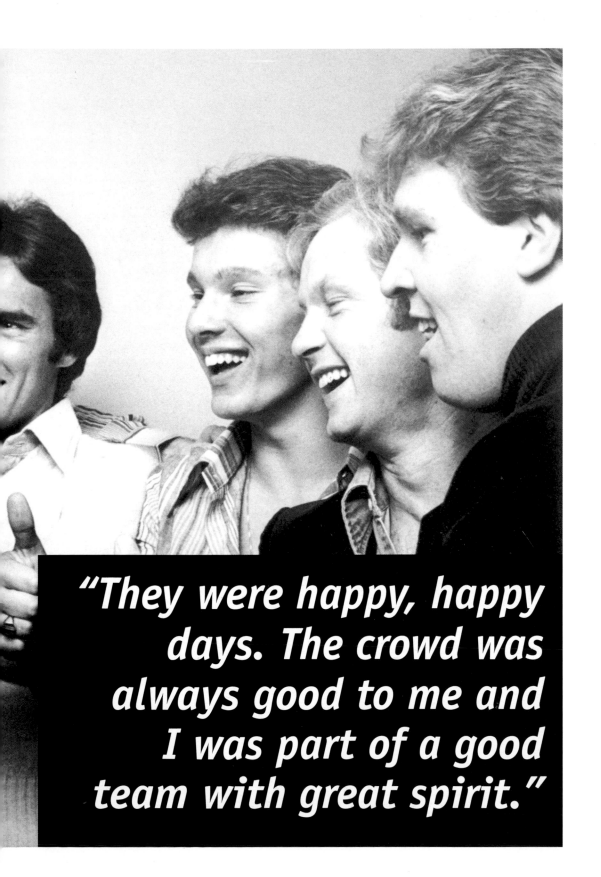

"They were happy, happy days. The crowd was always good to me and I was part of a good team with great spirit."

Doug Allder too, he put a lot of great crosses in for me. I knew where he'd deliver them and I could peel off the defender and attack the ball. Danis Salman had huge potential and good pace, but I don't think he really had the brain to go on and achieve things, I mean some players listen to advice and go on to the top, others don't.

When I was at Aldershot at the end of my career we had Teddy Sheringham down there on loan from Millwall. He was up to all sorts at the time, out on the piss the whole time, so I had a long chat with him and he went back to Millwall eventually and started scoring week in week out. I've worked it out that Teddy Sheringham is my only old team-mate still in the game."

Did you get on well with John Docherty?

"Yeah I think so. He had his own ideas on how he wanted to play and the players respected that. Training was always really tough with John, especially in the pre-season. He had some strange methods of making us work harder too, I remember, he'd have us in for normal training in the morning, then in the afternoon, he made us all do a cross country run.

It was always quite a long distance, but only the first ten would have a pint of bitter shandy waiting for them at the finish line. If you finished eleventh, you missed out. It was crazy. We were all so thirsty and there was all sorts of scrapping and pranks going on in an effort to get a good position at the front and a pint.

Some of the antics were pretty underhand too, I remember running alongside Gordon Sweetzer as we were approaching the final section and I asked him to slow down and help me out as I told him I wasn't feeling well and needed help.

But as he slowed down, I started to sprint and I got the final pint. He hit me for that afterwards."

But Gordon Sweetzer was your main striking partner when you arrived though. Did he forgive you?

"Yeah, it was all taken in good spirits. Gordon was a bit injury prone because he used to go in where it really hurt. I suppose I was a bit like that too, but he'd go in to some tackles where he shouldn't have and he used to pick up a lot of knocks in the process. He was a good player, but he wasn't experienced enough in certain aspects of the game, he used to think he was invincible. But you've got to be a bit clever sometimes."

There was a bit of a bust-up between the Board and Docherty at the start of the 1976-77 season over the team's poor start to the campaign. Docherty eventually resigned. How did this affect the team?

"I don't think it affected us much to be honest. I don't really remember it really affecting morale or anything, but then again, Bill Dodgin came in and he was such a lovely bloke. His personality would win anyone over. Bill had a good philosophy on the game. He always had us training with the ball, letting the ball do the work. He was a real character away from football too."

Other people have said that he loved to let his hair down off duty?

"[Laughs] He certainly did. I remember we had an evening over at Fox Hills golf course - he used to love golf - we went over there a lot. As we were coming out of the pub in Shepperton to make our way to the course in Chertsey, he called for my wife to get in his car.

We'd had a few drinks, everyone had really, there were no breath tests really back then and as we drove off he hit three cars as he bounced up the road.

I remember a fan called Brian Matthews, a big lad, a great supporter of Brentford, used to come out with us a lot. He used to work over at Fox Hills and all the players loved him. He used to tell wonderful jokes. Like Bill, sadly he died a few years ago."

What's your funniest recollection of the parties you went to with the other players?

"[Laughs] There was this bloke called John Murray who arrived from Reading. He wasn't a bad winger as it goes, but at every party he came to he always used to strip completely naked and

2002— McCulloch reflecting on happy days at Brentford

walk around. In the end it was just accepted as being almost normal that he was walking around without any clothes on.

He wasn't exactly gifted if you catch my drift, so we couldn't quite work out why he was doing it.

But I remember at one party he'd taken all his clothes off again and my wife tried to stop John Lyons' missus from walking in and getting a shock. But when she found out what was going on she shoved my wife out of the way so she could get an eyeful herself. It was hysterical."

You continued to score goals at a healthy rate after we'd won promotion, so it was no surprise to see other clubs coming in for you. How did the move to Sheffield Wednesday come about though?

"Well that's another strange story. I don't remember exactly what game it was, but I remember I'd gone in for this header and got clobbered by a defender or the 'keeper and I got knocked out. I came round but I was in no state to carry on, so they stretchered me off and took me to the dressing room to recover. I was still feeling really groggy when I looked up and saw Ian St. John, who was Wednesday's manager at the time. He said 'hello' and asked if I would be interested in a possible move to Sheffield. I didn't really know if I was hallucinating but said I'd consider it. I was fully conscious when I signed though."

What reception did you receive when you came back to Griffin Park as a Wednesday player for the 2-2 draw in 1979?

"I don't really remember that game much at all really. I don't think it was a very good match and I don't recall the reception I was given to be honest."

How do you look back at your time with Brentford?

"They were happy, happy days. The crowd was always good to me and I was part of a good team with great spirit. The social scene was the best I've known in the game. It was a great honour to be invited to the club's centenary celebrations in London in 1988. It was a very emotional night."

2001– Buttigieg enjoys a beer with his Brentford friend Paul Andrews

John Buttigieg

Date: Thursday May 24th, 2001
Venue: Staines Rugby Ground
Era: 1988-1992 Appearances: 47 Goals: 0

I suppose it was revolutionary at the time, even a bit exotic, for a struggling Third Division side like Brentford to be dabbling with International signings. But after tempting Stan Bowles and Chopper Harris to the home of world soccer (a.k.a. Griffin Park) John Buttigieg, Brentford's Maltese Falcon, seemed every bit as special back then.

Buttigieg was one of those players who pop up now and again and make you think "hold on a minute, this guy's a bit special, how come we've got him"?

Unfortunately these players don't last long. Either they're sold on quick, or more mysteriously, never get a real chance in the first team due to some dubious training ground run-in or a clash of personalities with the manager. Buttigieg definitely fitted the bill of a potential Griffin Park great, but unfortunately it obviously just wasn't meant to be.

Beesotted met up with John while he was visiting a Bees supporting pal who has stayed good friends with the player and who invited Buttigieg and his father over to London for his wedding.

How did your move to Brentford come about?

"I think Peter Shreeves spotted me playing for Malta in Northern Ireland and he must have talked to Steve Perryman while he was still at Spurs.

He eventually made contact with me when he joined Brentford and I was invited over to play in Brentford's pre-season tour of Portugal where I played very well I think.

I eventually joined Brentford in November '88 for £40,000."

Despite your obvious class, your time at Brentford didn't really work out for you though did it?

"No not really, I have some good memories though. There were several problems really, I was brought in to play as a sweeper, my natural position, but Steve Perryman decided to change the system after I arrived as the other players seemed to struggle with the style.

After Steve left, Phil Holder changed things even more and played the long-ball game, which certainly didn't suit players like me at all.

Phil was a good guy though; he was honest with me and told me that he would be changing the system. I went on loan to Swindon who were managed by Ossie Ardiles at the time, but I was only really cover for injuries.

But I'm glad I played in England, even for a short time."

Did Brentford treat you well?

"It's hard to say really. It was hard to be a foreigner at the club at the time. I am sure it is different for your Icelandic players now, but I did feel an outsider for a while. Joyce Neate at the club was lovely to me and some of the players too, but it was very hard for me I remember. I made good friends with some Brentford fans though."

Brentford enjoyed a fabulous Cup run that season, so was it frustrating to play just a bit part in the whole thing?

"Yes it was, but I played in the First Round game against Halesowen and have good memories of the matches against Manchester City, Blackburn and Liverpool. I was away on International duties for some of that time too, so my first team chances were reduced anyway.

We had some very good players at the time, Andy Sinton was a different class and Roger Joseph, Andy Feeley and Gary Blissett were all good players too. The problem was in defence really. Keith Millen and Terry Evans weren't at their best at that time."

Have you heard the 'urban myth' that suggests you had an affair with Steve Perryman's wife and that is why you weren't picked as often as you should have been?

"[Laughs] Yes I did hear that. Not until about three years ago, though, when I met some Brentford fans in a bar in Malta and

1989— Buttigieg during a pre-season friendly at Kingstonian

they told me about the story. They sang me the song that you sang after I left too, which I found very funny.

There is absolutely no truth in it at all though. I did stay at Steve's house for a short while, that's all, honestly!"

Did you have the chance to play abroad anywhere else?

"Yes, I did sign to play for a team in Germany, Rotweiss Essen, but they had financial troubles at the time and the League relegated them to the German Third Division. Clubs can't sign professional footballers at that level and my deal broke down."

You enjoyed a wonderful International career with Malta and must have some superb memories of your time in the game. What's the best atmosphere you can remember?

"Absolutely, International football is the best thing a player can enjoy and I have been fortunate to play all over the world and against some of the greatest players in the world too. The best atmosphere as far as I am concerned is at Lansdowne Road in Ireland, it's a great place to play and the crowd is fantastic."

But you've retired from the International scene now?

"Well yes, but I didn't want to finish on 97 caps. I wasn't treated well by the Maltese Association and wasn't allowed to reach 100 caps, which I feel I deserved. My final game was against England [2000] in the friendly before the European Championships in Holland and Belgium.

Malta had three other friendlies after the game with England and I should have been allowed to play, even as substitute, so I could have reached 100 caps. I was gutted, at 37 I feel I could have carried on for a while longer."

You are still playing club football though aren't you? Your current club, Valetta, have had a great season haven't they?

"Yes, it was a record-breaking season for a Maltese club. We only lost three matches all season and won all six domestic cup competitions. Nobody has done that before. We now qualify for the Champions League qualifying rounds."

Photo Information and Credits

<u>Page</u>   <u>Photographer/Agency/Newspaper</u>

Ken Coote
10-11   Unknown   Ken's personal collection
15   Paul Slattery
16   G.J. Reeves   Ken's personal collection
18-19   Middlesex Chronicle

Joe Allon
22-23   Middlesex Chronicle
26   Middlesex Chronicle
30-31   Middlesex Chronicle
36   David Lane

Terry Hurlock
38-39   Unknown
42   David Lane
44-45   David Lane

Alan Nelmes
50-51   MCT Sport
54   Paul Slattery
56-57   Brentford & Chiswick Times   Chiswick Library
61   Brentford & Chiswick Times   Chiswick Library
64   Paul Slattery

Doug Allder
70-71   Brentford & Chiswick Times   Chiswick Library
74   Paul Slattery
76-77   Ealing Gazette
83   Paul Slattery

Dean Holdsworth
88-89   Middlesex Chronicle
92   Middlesex Chronicle
95   Lee Doyle
96-97   Bill Grant
98   David Lane

Tommy Higginson
100-101   Middlesex Chronicle   Tommy's personal collection
104   Paul Slattery
106   Unknown   Tommy's personal collection
110   Middlesex Chronicle   Tommy's personal collection
116   Paul Slattery

Ivar Ingimarsson
118-119   Middlesex Chronicle
123   David Lane
124   Middlesex Chronicle

Andy Feeley
126-127   Reed Northern Newspapers
130   David Lane
132-133   Reed Northern Newspapers
136   David Lane

Andy McCulloch
138-139   Unknown   Andy's personal collection
143   Evening Mail
146-147   Unknown   Andy's personal collection
150   David Lane

John Buttigieg
152-153   David Lane
156   David Lane

Not even Joe Crozier can save Brentford these days . . .

. . . but with your help BEES UNITED can

"We're by far the greatest team, the world has ever seen...."